Men-at-Arms . 503

Hitler's Russian & Cossack Allies 1941–45

Nigel Thomas PhD • Illustrated by Johnny Shumate

Series editor Martin Windrow

First published in Great Britain in 2015 by Osprey Publishing
Kemp House, Chawley Park, Oxford OX2 9PH, UK
1385 Broadway, 5th Floor, New York, NY 10018, USA
29 Earlsfort Terrace, Dublin 2, Ireland

Osprey Publishing, part of Bloomsbury Publishing Plc

A CIP catalogue record for this book is available from the British Library

Print ISBN: 978 1 4728 0687 1
PDF ebook ISBN: 978 1 4728 0688 8
ePub ebook ISBN: 978 1 4728 0689 5

Editor: Martin Windrow
Index by Mark Swift
Typeset in Helvetica Neue and ITC New Baskerville
Originated by PDQ Media, Bungay, UK
Printed and bound in India by Replika Press Private Ltd.

21 22 23 24 25 10 9 8 7 6 5 4

www.ospreypublishing.com

Dedication

This book is respectfully dedicated to the memory of
Brian Leigh Davis (1935–2014)
whose work was an inspiration to us all.

Acknowledgements

Nigel Thomas would like to thank the correspondents whose interest, kindness and patience have contributed so much to this book: Dušan Babac, Nik Cornish, Christopher Harrod, Ventsislav Tchakov, and Pierre C.T. Verheye. In addition to sources listed in the Select Bibliography on page 40, the author would like to acknowledge the published works of the late Philip H. Buss, Dieter Deuster, S. Drobyazko and A. Karashchuk, William Greehey, Joachim Hoffmann, Rolf Michaelis, Antonio J. Muñoz, George F. Nafziger, Nikolai Tolstoy and Henry L. de Zeng IV.
He would also like to thank his wife Heather for her tireless encouragement and support.

For further information on Nigel Thomas or to contact him, please refer to his website nt-associates.com

Editor's note

For the sake of space, this text does not follow the usual MAA conventions for abbreviations. In the narrative text we adopt 'note form': e.g. we do not spell out the numbers for Armies; we abbreviate 'brigade', 'regiment', 'battalion', 'company', 'squadron' and 'battery' in general uses of those terms, and the names of some months are also abbreviated.

Note that the date abbreviations in tables follow British style – i.e. 1.2.43 = 1st February 1943.

Abbreviations used in the text and battle-order tables

Arty	artillery
Bde	brigade
Bn	battalion
Btl	Bataillon (German)
Cav	cavalry
Co	company
Div	division
Eng	engineer
Gds	Guards
Gren	grenadier (infantry)
Inf	infantry
Mot	motorized
Mtd	mounted
Recce	reconnaissance
Regt	regiment
Sigs	signals
sing.	singular
Sqn	squadron
Vol	volunteer
AA	anti-aircraft
AG	Army Group
AK	Polish Home Army
aka	also known as
AT	anti-tank
C.	Central
E.	East
FGR	Fortress Grenadier Regiment
GOC	General Officer Commanding
HJ	Hitler Youth
HQ	headquarters
KONR	Russian People's Liberation Committee
MG	machine gun
MP	Military Police
N.	North
NCO	non-commissioned officer
OC	Officer Commanding
OKH	German Army High Command
POW	prisoner (s) of war
Pz	Panzer (German armoured units)
RNNA	Russian Nationalist People's Army
ROA	Russian Liberation Army
RONA	Russian Liberation People's Army
ROVS	Russian All-Military Union
RSI	Italian Social Republic
S.	South
SD	SS Security Service
SVB	Autonomous District (in USSR)
UPA	Ukrainian Insurgent Army
UVV	Ukrainian Liberation Army
VS	Armed Forces
VVS	Air Force
W.	West
WO	warrant officer

HITLER'S RUSSIAN & COSSACK ALLIES 1941–45

INTRODUCTION

On 22 June 1941, 3.6 million German and Axis forces attacked the 2.9 million-strong Red Army along the 1,200-mile Soviet western border in the largest military offensive in history. Hitler planned to capture Moscow and Leningrad (now St Petersburg) and occupy most of the European USSR up to the Arkangelsk-Astrakhan Line. Army Group North would advance through the Baltic States and northern Russia to Leningrad, AG Centre was to occupy Belarus and central Russia, and AG South was to advance through Ukraine to Stalingrad (now Volgograd). However, determined Red Army resistance, unsurfaced roads and shocking weather halted the advance of AG North around Leningrad, and AG Centre was forced back before Moscow. Army Group South continued through Ukraine, dividing in July 1942 into AG 'A' heading for Stalingrad, and AG 'B' for the Caucasian oilfields.

By Nov 1942 the Wehrmacht had occupied about 750,000 square miles of Soviet territory, and huge numbers of Soviet citizens had joined the Germans to fight against Stalin's regime. Actual numbers are impossible to determine, but a total of at least 600,000 auxiliaries has been estimated, of whom perhaps half were armed troops. After the catastrophic German defeat at Stalingrad in Feb 1943 the Axis forces were condemned to almost continual retreat, and by Nov 1944 they had lost all the captured ground except the Baltic States. Nevertheless, tens of thousands of unlucky former Soviet personnel continued to serve until the very end of the war, on battlefields as diverse as Normandy and Croatia.

Seen beyond a 7.62mm M1928 Degtyaryov light machine gun, *GenLt* Andrey A. Vlasov, the nominal (but not operational) commander of the Russian Liberation Army (ROA), is photographed while inspecting an Eastern Battalion. He wears his 1943 dark grey uniform with the M1943 ROA cap badge (see Plate C2). Vlasov had been a talented, inspiring Soviet general, more personable than his severe appearance suggests, but almost three years of German prevarications demoralized him, and he was unable to act decisively when finally given control of the Russian People's Liberation Committee (KONR) divisions in Nov 1944. (Author's collection)

The occupation zones

Occupied Soviet territory was divided into four north-south zones, moving eastwards, expanding in width during the advances and narrowing during the retreats. The Western Zone, in theory pacified, formed two provinces (sing. *Reichskommissariat*) under German civilian administration: *Ostland* (Baltic States and Belarus) and *Ukraine* (Ukraine and southern Russia); and two incomplete provinces: *Moskau* (northern and central Russia) and *Kaukasus*.

The West-Central Zone comprised the Army Group Rear Area, with local police *(Schutzmannschaft)* and militias organized under AGs North, Centre, and South (later AGs 'A'/South Ukraine, 'B' and 'Don'/North Ukraine), each having a Rear Area GOC *(Befehlshaber des rückwärtigen Heeresgebiets*, abbreviated *Berück)*.

The East-Central Zone was the Army Rear Area, with second-line field army units under each Army's Rear Area

OC *(Kommandant des rückwärtigen Armeegebiets*, abbreviated *Korück*): AG North had *Korück* 583 (18th Army), 584 (16th) and 593, later 585 (4th Panzer Group); AG Centre comprised *Korück* 532 (2nd Pz Army, later 9th Army), 559 (4th), 580 (2nd), 582 (9th) and 590 (3rd Pz); AG South and its successors had *Korück* 531 (1st Pz), 550 (17th), 553 (11th), 585, later 593 (6th), and 595, later 558 (8th Army).

The Eastern zone comprised the Operational Area *(Operationsgebiet)*, eventually held by 13 Armies and Pz Groups (later Pz Armies). Soviet pro-German forces operated in both the Army Group and Army Rear Areas, and often in the Operational Area.

Local recruitment

There were nine categories of Soviet volunteers in the Wehrmacht. This text covers six of those categories: Army auxiliaries *(Hilfswillige)*, Security units, Russian Liberation Army (ROA) Eastern Battalions and Luftwaffe, Russian People's Liberation Committee (KONR), independent Russian volunteer units, and Cossacks. Three categories – the Ukrainian Liberation Army (*Ukrainske Vyzvolne Viysko* – UVV), the Eastern Legions, and the Russian Corps in Serbia (including the 'Varyag' Volunteer Regiment) – are not examined; nor (apart from one – see page 17) are those raised by the Police, SS or Todt Organization labour corps.

Soviet citizens joined the German forces for a variety of reasons. Some were from non-Russian nationalities dreaming of independent statehood; others were anti-Communist Russians determined to overthrow Stalin. Many were pragmatic opportunists who simply wished to protect their villages, or to avoid death by starvation in German POW camps. The Germans' recruitment policy was driven by frontline Wehrmacht officers, who used subtle forms of persuasion to lead the fanatically anti-Russian Hitler along a path that his every political instinct rejected. On 6 Oct 1941 the recruitment of Soviet citizens became official German policy, under the designations Eastern Troops *(Osttruppen)* or Native Units *(landeseigene Verbände)*. From 1 Jan 1944, when 'East' had become a derogatory term, they were renamed Volunteer Units *(Freiwilligenverbände)*.

On 15 Dec 1942, GenLt Heinz Hellmich was appointed to the administrative post of Inspector of Eastern Troops at Army High Command *(Inspekteur der Osttruppen im OKH)*, redesignated GOC *(Genera*

Two Latvian *Hilfswillige*, posing with their womenfolk in autumn 1941. One man (3rd left) wears a Latvian Army M1930 khaki field cap without insignia, and an M1932 field tunic without collar patches or shoulder straps. A former Red Army soldier (right foreground) has an M1935 khaki field shirt without collar patches, an enlisted ranks' belt and khaki *sharovary* breeches. Both men have been awarded the General Assault Badge for participating in three separate attacks. The other three men are probably civilians. (Bundesarchiv, Bild 101I-004-3632-24/Elle/CC-BY-SA)

der Osttruppen im OKH) in early 1943. This ineffectual officer was succeeded on 1 Jan 1944 by the more dynamic Gen Ernst-August Köstring as General of Volunteer Units *(General der Freiwilligenverbände im OKH)*. Nevertheless, the real inspiration proved to be the charismatic captured Russian general Andrey A. Vlasov.

EASTERN TROOPS

Hilfswillige

From July 1941 German divisional commanders, facing mounting casualties, began accepting Soviet volunteers out of military and logistical necessity. Prisoners of war and deserters were employed as interpreters, wagon and lorry drivers, cooks, medical orderlies, ammunition carriers and messengers in German sub-units, while civilians joined supply units and construction battalions. Prisoners in Red Army uniforms stripped of Soviet insignia carried out fatigue duties in German units.

In Sept 1941 Hitler reluctantly agreed to allow recruitment of Soviet citizens as unarmed Voluntary Assistants (sing. *Hilfswilliger*, abbreviated *Hiwi*) in numbers up to 15 per cent of a division's strength (about 2,500 men) in Rear Areas, but soon armed Hiwis in numbers in excess of authorized limits were serving in combat units. For example, 134th Inf Div in 2nd Pz Army comprised 50 per cent Hiwis in late 1942, while 6th Army defended Stalingrad with 25 per cent Hiwis. A few discrete Hiwi units, such as Hiwi Ersatz Bataillon (depot bn) 46, were formed later in the war. By 1944 the German Army contained at least 600,000 Hiwis, including female medical officers and nurses. German attitudes towards them varied from hostility to admiration; for their part the Hiwis, with everything to lose if they returned to Soviet lines, usually served loyally.

Hiwi recruits wore Red Army uniforms without Soviet insignia, civilian clothes, or German Army uniforms without breast-eagles, collar patches or shoulder straps, but from 1 Oct 1941 an armband identifying their Wehrmacht service was worn on the left upper sleeve. After two months' probationary service German uniforms, insignia and ranks were permitted. Veteran Hiwis were indistinguishable from German troops, so Russians in 352nd Volks Gren Div in Normandy were ordered on 25 Apr 1944 to wear a white St Andrew's Cross on a field-grey patch on their cap, collar patches and shoulder straps. Army Order HV 44B Nr. 289 (later Nr. 292) of 1 Jul 1944 awarded Hiwis, now designated Volunteers, the same status as Germans, with promotion theoretically possible to *Unteroffizier* (corporal); local German commanders may have ignored this limitation, and doctors and veterinary surgeons could achieve field rank.

Security units, 1941–42

From Aug 1941, Army Group and Army commanders formed Russians and some Ukrainians and Belarusians into regiment- and battalion-sized Security Units *(Sicherungsverbände)* with locally coined titles, to patrol Army Rear Areas and confront the growing threat posed by the Soviet partisan movement. Meanwhile, locally raised police and militia sponsored by the SS and Police chain of command patrolled the Army Group Rear Areas.

Members of a Russian Security Bn emerge from a dugout before beginning a patrol in a Belarus forest, autumn 1942. They wear obsolete German M1916 helmets, Red Army M1935 khaki field shirts with M1942 red Security Bn collar patches and shoulder straps, *sharovary* breeches and marching boots. A medical orderly (far right) displays a red-cross armband. (Courtesy Central Museum of the Armed Forces, Moscow, via Stavka)

With the Baltic States virtually free of partisans, AG North's area was comparatively peaceful, forming 14 Security Bns (sing. *Sicherungs-Abteilung*). Korück 583 formed 11 such bns: 181–186 Estonian; 187 Volga Finnish (Mari, Mordvin); 188, 189, 410 & 510 Russian. These units fought on the Volkhov Front in Feb 1942. Meanwhile, Korück 584 formed an Anti-Partisan Light Bn *(Partisanjäger-Abteilung)* in 1942, with 6 rifle cos and an artillery bty, expanded on 2 Oct 1942 into Irregular Light Regt *(Freijäger-Regiment)* 16.

Army Group Centre, confronting huge numbers of Red Army stragglers fighting as partisans in the forests and swamps of Belarus, organized 66 battalions. Korück 532 had the most active area, forming up to 46 Volunteer Bns numbered I–XXXXVI. From these were formed Volunteer Regt 'Weise' (OC Maj Weise), later Volunteer Regt 'Dessna'. Other units raised were three Lokot Autonomous District (*Selbstverwaltungsbezirks* – SVB) People's Militia *(Miliz)*, later People's Defence Force *(Volksheer)* bns under Bronisław V. Kaminski, and two Volunteer Security *(Freiwilliges Sicherungs)* Bns: 'Hetman', later 134, and 447. Korück 559 raised the Bn von Hopfgarten and Self-Defence *(Selbstschutz)* Bn 456, and XII Corps Battalion. Korück 580 simply attached Eastern Companies to 581st MP (*Feldgendarmerie*) Bn and 581st Guard (*Wach*) Battalion. Korück 582 organized an Intervention Group under Oblt Georg Tietjen *(Eingreifsgruppe Tietjen)* with 6 Russian cos, which fought at Rzhev in Feb 1942; this was later reorganized into I–III/582 Volunteer Battalions. Berück Mitte formed the Hohlfeld Special HQ *(Sonderstab Hohlfeld)*; later, the Eastern Replacement Regt *(Ost-Ersatz Regiment)*, with 5 bns named after local rivers, under 203rd Security Div; and Russian Nationalist People's Army (RNNA) Experimental Bns (sing. *Versuchs-Bataillon*) 1–5. Army Group South mainly formed Cossack units as reinforcements, with only one other unit, Korück 585's 6th Ukrainian Bn, confirmed.

1943: young members of a Security Bn watch an older soldier consulting a map with a company sergeant-major from the unit's German cadre. The German wears an M1943 peaked field cap, M1935 tunic with *Oberfeldwebel* shoulder straps, NCO collar braid, and *Hauptfeldwebel* cuff rings. The Russians have M1942 enlisted ranks' field caps without badges, and M1940 tunics with German shoulder straps and collar patches but no breast-eagles. Note both Soviet PPSh41 and German MP40 sub-machine guns, and (right foreground) the 'quiff' hairstyle at the temple, the green buttonhole-ribbon of the Eastern Decoration in Bronze and the black Wound Badge. (Tchakov Collection)

These units had no standard organization, but normally comprised about 700 men in an HQ and 4 rifle bns, with 4 rifle cos each of 4 platoons. German officers and NCOs, in standard uniforms, provided the bn and most co and platoon commanders and a specialist NCO cadre.

Security unit uniforms and insignia

Initially Russian volunteers wore Hiwi uniforms, but Regulation 8000/42 of 20 Aug 1942 (possibly confirming a June 1942 order) prescribed German M1940 or captured uniforms, with bright red collar patches with silver (usually German NCO) braid edging, red shoulder straps, and German positional titles. The few Russian officers had silver-braid collar-patch edging and bars, silver German four-point rank stars, M1939 Specialist Officer *(Sonderführer)* narrow silver-wire shoulder straps, and gold rank knots. A *Zugführer* (effectively a senior NCO) wore two vertical (i.e. lengthways) silver braids on enlisted ranks' shoulder straps. Other NCOs and men wore silver-braid collar 'chevrons' (L-shaped sections of NCO braid) and rank bars, and red shoulder straps with 3–0 horizontal (i.e. transverse) braid bars. An NCO acting as *Hauptfeldwebel* (the company sergeant-major appointment) followed German practice by wearing two silver NCO-braid rings round both cuffs. The German breast-eagle above the right pocket was replaced by a light grey diamond-format swastika between long, shallow 'wings' on a field-grey backing. From 11 Nov 1942 enlisted ranks' shoulder straps were field-grey piped in bright red. Under Regulation 15 Nov 1942 (published 12 Dec 1942), officers wore the M1938 peakless field cap (sidecap) and other ranks the M1934 or M1942 cap, with a badge comprising a bright red vertical bar on a dark bluish-green cloth oval. The German helmet bore no insignia.

Eastern Battalions, 1942–43

On 12 July 1942, GenLt Andrey Andreyevich Vlasov, commanding the Red Army's élite 2nd Shock Army, was captured on the Volkhov Front in northern Russia. While in captivity, Vlasov, encouraged by sympathetic German officers, agreed to head a Russian anti-Communist movement. The Germans valued Vlasov's appeals to Soviet POWs to fight Stalin, but downplayed his ambition to create a democratic, post-Communist Russia.

From 23 Oct 1942, the Security Units (of which our Table 1, page 9-10, identifies 81) were reorganized as 50 numbered Eastern Bns *(Ost-Bataillone)*. Of these, 13 (653, 658–669) were under AG North; AG Centre had 36 units (134, 308, 406, 412, 427, 439, 446/82, I/447, II/447, 456, 601–605, 615–621, 627–630, 633–637, 642, 647–649 & 680); and one (551/651) came under AGs 'A' and 'B'. As the Germans retreated after Stalingrad a further 25 were formed: 4 under AG North (7, 550, 561 & 674); 17 with AG Centre (I/1 Guards Bde, 82, 229, 263, 268, 448/339, 441, 449, 553, 556, 560, 561, 600, 643, 646, 675 & 681); 3 (454, 555 & 559) in AGs 'A', 'B' and 'Don'; and 1 (752) in northern France. Most

Vlasov addresses soldiers of an *Ostbataillon* in 1943. They wear M1935 helmets without insignia; M1935 or M1940 tunics with respectively dark bluish-green, or field-grey, collars and shoulder straps. Some wear German M1940 collar patches and breast-eagles, but most display the Eastern Troops' M1942 red collar patches and shoulder straps, with silver-braid rank insignia. They have M1935 belts and ammunition pouches, and Karabiner 98k rifles. (Tchakov Collection)

Eastern Bns comprised mainly Russian, but also some Ukrainian and Belarusian *Freiwillige*. Here a Belarusian volunteer, Vassiliy Kigorovitsy, wears a German M1934 enlisted ranks' field cap with an M1943 ROA officers' red-blue oval cockade with silver sunrays, but retains above this (against regulations) a German Army M1935 light grey woven eagle-and-swastika on dark green backing. On the German M1943 tunic he displays regulation M1943 ROA enlisted ranks' dark bluish-green collar patches, with a silver button and braid centre-stripe. (Author's collection)

were infantry, but there were at least 10 specialist units: 555 Guard; 621 & 752 Artillery; 550 Ordnance; 454, 601, 605 & 666 Engineer; 559 Construction, and 651 Supply. Security Bn uniforms and insignia continued to be worn.

A 754-strong Eastern Bn had 78 German personnel (8 officers, 1 paymaster, 39 NCOs & 30 men), and 676 Eastern troops (5 officers, 81 NCOs & 590 men) in a 111-strong HQ, 3x 131-strong rifle cos, and a 151-man heavy MG company.

A large number of Eastern Cos were also formed, either as cos within German bns or as independent sub-units. In all, 424 of these Eastern Cos have been identified: 69 Eastern (infantry), 17 Guard, 34 Territorial Rifles, 3 Armoured, 10 Artillery, 3 Engineers, 1 Mine-Clearance, 125 Construction, 15 Road Construction, 11 Rail Construction, 21 Ordnance, 7 Signals, 21 Technical, 74 Supply, and 13 Transport.

General Vlasov was denied direct command over the Hiwis and Eastern Bns, but his propaganda value alone advanced his anti-Communist cause, especially after his Russian Committee published a 'Smolensk Declaration' leaflet of 13 Jan 1943 encouraging all Russians to rise up against Stalin.

Russian Liberation Army (ROA), 1943–44

In Feb 1943 the Eastern Bns – whether composed of Russians, Ukrainians or Belarusians – were issued an arm shield for the left upper sleeve. This displayed the Cyrillic yellow letters 'POA' (in Roman, 'ROA', standing for Russian Liberation Army, *Russkaya Osvoboditel'naya Armiya*) above the traditional Russian St Andrew's Cross (blue saltire on a white shield, edged red), all on a black sheild. This badge was a cynical ploy by the Germans to retain Russian loyalty and encourage hope for a Russian anti-Communist army, which Hitler had expressly vetoed. The ROA remained a series of independent battalions and companies under German command, unable to cooperate with each other or to accept Vlasov's orders.

From Jan 1943, Army Group commanders had been discreetly organizing 13 regimental staffs to supervise the Eastern Bns, but Hitler's intransigence prevented their development. Initially these staffs were designated OC Eastern Troops *(Kommandeur der Osttruppen)*, numbered

France, summer 1944: men of an Eastern Bn attempt a sing-song, apparently with little enthusiasm. The group shows slight variations of German uniform: M1942 field caps with M1943 ROA red-blue oval badges on the crown; M1941 or M1943 tunics with M1940 collar patches, and M1935 or M1940 shoulder straps with infantry-white piping; M1940 breast-eagles (permitted from 15 April 1944), and the M1943 ROA arm shield. The *Yefreytor* in the foreground wears the M1943 shoulder-strap rank bar. (Bundesarchiv, Bild 101I-297-1704-10/Müller, Karl/ CC-BY-SA)

Table 1: Russian Liberation Army battalions, 24 Aug 1941–8 May 1945

Eastern Battalions:

- Estonian Security Bn 181 (raised 8.1941, in N. Russia); 23.10.1942, became (Estonian) Eastern Bn 658; 6.1944, disbanded
- Estonian Security Bn 182 (r. 8.1941, N. Russia); 23.10.1942, (Estonian) Eastern Bn 659; 6.1944, disbanded
- Estonian Security Bn 183 (r. 20.8.1941, N. Russia); 23.10.1942, (Russian) Eastern Bn 661; 11.1943, S. France; 19.4.1944, IV Bn/Reserve Gren Regt 239, S. France; 11.1944, disbanded
- Estonian Security Bn 184 (r. 8.1941, N. Russia); 23.10.1942, (Estonian) Eastern Bn 660; 6.1944, disbanded
- Estonian Security Bn 185 (r. 9.1941, N. Russia); 23.10.1942, (Russian) Eastern Bn 662; 12.1943, Denmark; 30.4.1944, III Bn/Gren Regt 712; 22.6.1944, III (Russian) Bn/Gren Regt 712; 9.1944, (Russian) Eastern Bn 662; 4.1945, (Russian) Gren Regt 1605, Denmark
- Hetman Bn 134 (r. 1942, C. Russia); 1942, Volunteer Security Bn 134; 18.11.1942, Eastern Bn 134, C. Russia; 27. 11.1943, disbanded
- Dnjepr Eastern Combat Bn (r. 29.4.1942, C. Russia); 23.10.1942, Dnjepr Eastern Bn 602; 5.11.1943, N. France; 17.8.1944, destroyed, W. France
- Beresina Eastern Combat Bn (r. 1.6.1942, C. Russia); 23.10.1942, Beresina Eastern Bn 601; 5.1943, Eastern Eng Bridging Bn 601, S. France; 13.7.1944, Russian Eng Bridging Bn 601; 10.1944, to 600 Russian Inf Div, W. Germany
- Ukrainian Bn 6 (r. 17.6.1942, S. Russia); 30.11.1942, Eastern Bn 551; 1.2.1944, Eastern Supply Bn 651; 1945, Ukrainian Supply Bn 651, W. Germany
- VI Volunteer Bn (r. 6.1942, C. Russia); 11.1.1943, Eastern Bn 406; 28.9.1943, S. France; 6.7.1944, Russian Bn 406; 9.1944, N. Italy
- XXIII Vol Bn (r. 6.1942, C. Russia); 8.11.1942, Eastern Bn 308; late 1944, Russian Bn 308, Poland; 2.1945, to 600 Russian Inf Div, W. Germany
- XXVIII Vol Bn (r. 6.1942, C. Russia); 8.11.42, Eastern Bn 427; 1.10.1944, E. Germany; 2.1945, to 600 Russian Inf Div, W. Germany
- XXXIX Vol Bn (r. 6.1942, C. Russia); 8.11.1942, Eastern Bn 439; 10.1943, N. France; 19.4.1944, IV (Eastern) Bn/Gren Regt 726; 8.1944, E. France; 10.1944, disbanded
- XXXXVI Vol Bn (r. 6.1942, C. Russia); 8.11.1942, Eastern Bn 446; 15.1.1943, re-formed; 5.1944, disbanded
- People's Militia Bn Trutschevsk (r. 21.6.1942, C. Russia); later, People's Defence Bn Trutschevsk; 18.11.1942, Eastern Bn 618; 10.1943, Belarus; 11.1943, N. France; 19.4.1944, re-formed as mot bn; 11.1944, to 600 Russian Inf Div, W. Germany
- People's Militia Bn Dmitrovsk (r. 21.6.1942, C. Russia); later, People's Defence Bn Dmitrovsk; 18.11.1942, Eastern Bn 619; 6.1943, Training Bn; 11.1943, disbanded
- People's Militia Bn Kromy (r. 21.6.1942, C. Russia); later, People's Defence Bn Kromy; 18.11.1942, Eastern Bn 620, C. Russia; 8.1943, Belarus; 11.1943, N. Italy; 2.1944, II Bn/Gren Regt 274; 3.1945, Russian Bn 620
- Estonian Security Bn 186 (r. summer 1942, N. Russia); 23.10.1942, (Russian) Eastern Bn 663; 12.1943, S. France; 19.4.1944, I Bn/Gren Regt 759; 9.1944, almost destroyed; 2.1945, to 600 Russian Inf Div, W. Germany
- Finnish Security Bn 187 (r. summer 1942, N. Russia); 23.10.1942, (Finnish) Eastern Bn 664; 1944, disbanded
- Russian Security Bn 188 (r. summer 1942, N. Russia); 23.10.1942, (Russian) Eastern Bn 665; 10.1943, S. France; 19.4.1944, III (Eastern) Bn/Fortress Gren Regt 757; 9.1944, disbanded
- Russian Security Bn 410 (r. summer 1942, N. Russia); 23.10.1942, Eastern Bn 653; 12.1943, Denmark; 30.4.1944, II Bn/(Eastern) Gren Regt 714; 22.6.1944,II Bn/(Russian) Gren Regt 714; 4.1945, II Bn/(Russian) Gren Regt 1604, Denmark
- Russian Security Bn 510 (r. summer 1942, N. Russia); 23.10.1942, Eastern Bn 654; 10.1943, S. France; 21.10.1944, to Waffen-SS Inf Regt 77
- Russian Security Bn 189 (r. summer 1942, N. Russia); 23.10.1942, (Russian) Eastern Eng Bn 666; 10.1943, S. France; 19.4.1944, IV (Eastern) Bn/FGR 932; 21.7.1944, IV (Russian) Bn/Gren Regt 932; 8.1944, S. France; 10.1944, to 600 Russian Inf Div, W. Germany
- Düna Eastern Combat Bn (r. 4.7.1942, C. Russia); 30.9.1942, Düna Eastern Bn 603; 12.1943, Denmark; 30.4.1944, I Bn/(Eastern) Gren Regt 714; 22.6.1944, I Bn/(Russian) Gren Regt 714; 4.1945, I Bn/(Russian) Gren Regt 1604, Denmark
- Wolga Eastern Combat Bn (r. 9.7.1942, C. Russia); 5.10.1942, Wolga Eastern Bn 605; 11.1943, N. France; 14.12.1943, Eastern Eng Bridging Bn 605; 13.7.1944, Russian Eng Bridging Bn 605, N. France; 2.1945, to 600 Russian Inf Div, W. Germany
- Pripjet Eastern Combat Bn (r. 14.7.1942, C. Russia); 30.9.1942, Pripjet Eastern Bn 604; 5.1943, disbanded
- I/582 Vol Bn (r. 30.9.1942, C. Russia); 19.11.1942, Eastern Bn 628; 11.1943, Belgium; 19.4.1944, I (Eastern) Bn/Gren Regt 745; 9–11.1944, Belgium & Netherlands; 13.12.1944, to 600 Russian Inf Div, W. Germany
- II/582 Vol Bn (r. 30.9.1942, C. Russia); 19.11.1942, Eastern Bn 629; 10.1943, Belarus; 25.11.1943, N. France; 19.4.1944, IV (Eastern) Bn/Gren Regt 899; 29.9.1944, disbanded
- III/582 Vol Bn (r. 30.9.1942, C. Russia); 19.11.1942, Eastern Bn 630; 15.10.1943, Belarus; 1.12.1943, N. France; 19.4.1944, I (Eastern) Bn/FGR 857; 12.1944, to 600 Russian Inf Div, W. Germany
- I Bn/Irregular Light Regt 16 (r. 2.10.1942, N. Russia); 14.1.1943, Eastern Bn 667; 12.1943, Denmark; 30.4.1944, III Bn/(Eastern) Gren Regt 714; 22.6.1944, III Bn/(Russian) Gren Regt 714; 4.1945, III Bn/(Russian) Gren Regt 1604, Denmark
- II Bn/Irregular Light Regt 16 (r. 2.10.1942, N. Russia); 14.1.1943, Eastern Bn 668; 11.1943, Schnittenheim Eastern Bn; 17.12.1943, disbanded
- III Bn/Irregular Light Regt 16 (r. 3.1942, N. Russia); 2.10.1942, III Bn/Irregular Light Regt; 14.1.1943, Eastern Bn 669; 11.1943, Belgium; 6.7.1944, Russian Bn 669, Belgium; 9.3.1945, to ROA, W. Germany
- 4–6, later 7 (Eastern) Cos/MP Bn 581 (r. 9.10.1942, C. Russia); 12.9.1943, Eastern Bn 649; 11.1943, N. France; 19.4.1944, IV (Eastern) Bn/FGR 729; 7.1944, disbanded
- I Bn/Vol Regt 'Dessna' (r. 5.10.1942, C. Russia); 18.11.1942, Eastern Bn 615; 10.1943, N. France; 10.1944, destroyed, E. France
- II Bn/Vol Regt 'Dessna' (r. 5.10.1942, C. Russia); 18.11.1942, Eastern Bn 616; 11.1943, N. Italy; 1944, III (Eastern) Bn/Gren Regt 194; 1.1945, Russian Bn 616, N. Italy
- III Bn/Vol Regt 'Dessna' (r. 5.10.1942, C. Russia); 18.11.1942, Eastern Bn 617; 11.1943, N. Italy; 7.1944, Russian Bn 617; 4.1945, disbanded
- Vol Arty Bn 'Dessna' (r. 5.10.1942, C. Russia); 18.11.1942, Eastern Arty Bn 621; 12.1943, N. France; 28.10.1944, to E. Germany; 3.1945, Arty Regt 1650, 650 Russian Inf Div, W. Germany
- Self-Defence Bn 456 (r. 1942, C. Russia); 11.1942, Eastern Bn 456; 6.1943, 4–9 Eastern Security Cos/Security Bn 456; 17.10.1943, Eastern Co 456; 4.12.1943, to Eastern Bn 617
- Vol Security Bn 447 (r. 12.1942, C. Russia); 15.1.1943, Eastern Bns I/447 & II/447; 2.1944, disbanded
- Eastern Bn 263 (r. winter 1942, C. Russia); 12.1943, N. Italy; 4.1945, disbanded
- Von Hopfgarten Bn (r. winter 1942, C. Russia); 15.1.1943, Eastern Bn 642; 11.1943, N. France; 19.4.1944, IV (Eastern) Bn/Gren Regt 736; 4.1945, Russian Bn 642, W. Germany
- 4–10 (Eastern) Cos/Guard Bn 581 (r. winter 1942, C. Russia); 12.9.1943, Eastern Bn 647; formation doubtful.
- 8 & 9 (Eastern) Cos/Guard Bn 581 (r. winter 1942, C. Russia); summer 1943, 8 & 9 (Eastern) Cos/Security Bn 456; 12.9.1943, Eastern Bn 648, Belarus; 27.11.1943, disbanded
- 12 Corps Self-Defence Bn (r. late 1942, C. Russia); 13.1.1943, Eastern Bn 412; 12.1943, III Bn/Gren Regt 578, N. Italy; 3.1945, Russian Bn 412, N. Italy

(Continued overleaf)

Table 1: Russian Liberation Army battalions, 24 Aug 1941–8 May 1945 (cont.)

- Eastern Bn 448 (r. 12.1942, S. Russia); 1.1943, Eastern Bn 339; 12.1943, N. Italy; 1944, III Bn/Gren Regt 871; 2.1945, Russian Bn 339, N. Italy
- Cossack Sqn 559 (r. 1942, C. Russia); 12.1942, Eastern Bn 627; 10.1943, N. France; 7.12.1943, Volga Tartar Bn 627; 1.7.1944, disbanded after mutiny; 7.1944, Eastern Bn 627, N. France; 1945, W. Germany
- RNNA Experimental Bn 1 (r. 5.1942, C. Russia); 1.1943, Eastern Bn 633; 11.1943, N. France; 19.4.1944, IV (Eastern) Bn/FGR 852; 9.1944, surrendered, Brest
- RNNA Experimental Bn 2 (r. 5.1942, C. Russia); 1.1943, Eastern Bn 634; 11.1943, N. France; 19.4.1944, III (Eastern) Bn/FGR 895; 1944, destroyed, Normandy
- RNNA Experimental Bn 3 (r. 5.1942, C. Russia); 1.1943, Eastern Bn 635; 11.1943, N. France; 6.1944, destroyed.
- RNNA Experimental Bn 4 (r. 9.1942, C. Russia); 1.1943, Eastern Bn 636; 11.1943, N. France; 10.5.1945, surrendered, W. France
- RNNA Experimental Bn 5 (r. 9.1942, C. Russia); 1.1943, Eastern Bn 637; 1945, E. Germany
- Eastern Bn 82 (r. 15.1.1943 from Eastern Bn 446, C. Russia); summer 1943, disbanded
- Eastern Bn 229 (r. 15.1.1943, C. Russia); 2.1944, disbanded
- Eastern Bn 441 (r. 15.1.1943, C. Russia); 19.1.1944, N. France; 6.1944, destroyed
- Eastern Guard Bn 555 (r. 15.1.1943, E. Germany); 2.1943, S. Russia; 12.1943, N. Italy; 1.1944, III Bn/Gren Regt 755; 1.1945, Russian Bn 555; 5.1945, surrendered
- Eastern Bn 556 (r. 15.1.1943, C. Russia); 1944, N. Italy; 28.3.1944, III Bn/Gren Regt 955; 20.6.1944, Russian Bn 556, N. Italy; 5.1945, surrendered
- Convalescent Bn Russia (r. 18.1.1943); 30.4.1943, I, & 1.6.1943, II (Eastern People's) Convalescent Bns, Generalgouvernement; 25.1.1944, disbanded, formed Convalescent Bn/Eastern Replacement Regt & Eastern People's Security Bn 553
- Eastern Construction Bn, GOC Southern Command (r. 15.1.1943, Ukraine); 26.3.1943, Eastern Construction Bn 559; 19.8.1943, Eastern Construction Eng Bn 559; 1945, E. Germany
- Eastern Bn 643 (r. 23.3.1943, C. Russia); 10.1943, N. France; 19.4.1944, IV Bn/Gren Regt 582; 9.5.1945, surrendered, Jersey
- Eastern Engineer Bn 454 (r. 20.4.1943, Ukraine); 5.8.1944, disbanded
- Eastern Bn Hansen (r. 29.4.1943, C. Russia); 23.10.1943, Eastern Bn 681; 19.4.1944, IV (Russian) Bn/Gren Regt 934, S. France; 8.1944, Eastern Bn 681, W. Germany; 2.1945, to 600 Russian Inf Div, W. Germany
- IV/Drushina SS Regt (r. 5.1943, Belarus); 6.1943, I Bn, 1 ROA Guards Bde, C. Russia; 11.1943, disbanded
- Eastern Ordnance Bn 550 (r. 5.1943, C. Russia); 1.1944, N. Russia; 9.6.1944, Ukrainian Ordnance Bn 550, Vol Depot Regt 3, S. France
- Welcker Eastern Bn (r. 16.6.1943, N. Russia); 21.10.1943, (Russian) Eastern Bn 674; 12.1943, Denmark; 4.1944, IV Bn/Reserve Gren Regt 6; 1945, Russian Bn 674; 4.1945, (Russian) Gren Regt 1605, Denmark
- Eastern Bn 268 (r. summer 1943, C. Russia); 2.1944, disbanded
- Eastern Bn 600 (r. summer 1943, C. Russia); 11.1943, N. France; 1945, Russian Bn 600, W. Germany, to Russian 650 Inf Div
- Eastern Bn 646 (r. summer 1943, C. Russia); 2.1944, disbanded (formation doubtful)
- 4–7 (East) Cos/Security Bn 456 (r. C. Russia); 12.9.1943, Eastern Bn 680; 11.1943, N. France; 1944, destroyed
- Eastern Bn 449 (r. late 1943, C. Russia); 2.1944, disbanded (formation doubtful)
- Eastern Arty Bn 752 (r. 23.12.1943, N. France); 8.1944, almost destroyed; 10.1944, to 600 Russian Inf Div, W. Germany
- Eastern People's Security Bn 553 (r. 25.1.1944, Generalgouvernement); 15.6.1944, Ukrainian Security Bn 553; 24.6.1944, Russian Security Bn 553; 12.1944, to ROA, W. Germany
- Eastern Bn 560 (r. 1.1944, N. Italy); 6.6.1944, III (Eastern) Bn/Gren Regt 1059; 31.7.1944, III (Eastern) Bn/Gren Regt 147; 1.1945, Russian Bn 560
- Eastern Bn 561 (r. 1.1944, Belarus); 1.2.1944, N. France; 6.1944, destroyed, N. France
- Eastern Bn 675 (r. 8.1944); 2.1945, to 600 Russian Inf Div, W. Germany
- Eastern Bn 7 (r. 12.1944, Poland); 4.1945, Russian Bn 7, E. Germany

582, 700–704, 710–712, 720, 721, 741 & Generalgouvernement (i.e. German-occupied Poland); but in Sept 1943–1944, six were redesignated Eastern Regimental Headquarters (sing. *Ost-Regiments-Stab*), numbered 580, 750–753 & 755.

ROA uniforms and insignia

The ROA continued to wear German field-grey uniforms, but new insignia, reminiscent of pre-Communist Russian uniforms, were introduced under Regulation Nr. 141242/43 of 29 May 1943, although they may have been in use as early as Jan 1943. Officers initially wore a red oval painted-metal cap badge with a surround of blue sunrays, but this was soon replaced by a red-blue oval with silver sunrays; NCOs and men had a red-blue oval only.

General officers wore tongue-shaped dark bluish-green collar patches with gold cord edge-piping and a horizontal gold braid with a plain gold pebbled button; field and subaltern officers had the same patch but with silver distinctions; NCOs and men the same, without the silver piping. Officers wore dark bluish-green or field-grey shoulder straps shaped like Tsarist *pogoni*, piped red; generals had gold zigzag braid and 2–0 silver four-point stars; field officers had two lengthways red stripes with 2–0 silver stars; subalterns wore the same but with one red centre-stripe. Non-commissioned officers and men wore pointed shoulder straps piped red, with 3–0 silver-braid transverse bars; on 1 Jan 1944, two 'seniority' ranks were introduced for men, incorporating a shoulder-strap star. Officers had been awarded Russian military rank titles under Regulation Nr. 1200/43, but NCOs and men used German ranks, with different titles in cavalry and artillery units. All ranks wore the M1943 ROA arm shield, but the M1942 'winged swastika' breast badge was discontinued. Suggestions that some ROA personnel wore a Russian field shirt *(gymnastiorka)* in French 'horizon-blue' are unconfirmed.

Transfers to the West

As the Wehrmacht retreated after Stalingrad the previously modest level of desertions and mutinies amongst the 74 ROA bns began to increase, prompting Hitler to order their transfer to France and northern Italy in Sept 1943. In fact only 46 bns left the Eastern Front, leaving 20 (82, 134, 229, 268, 446, 449, 454, 456, 604, 619, 646–648, 658–660, 664, 668, I/447 & II/447) to fight on there until their eventual destruction. Eight more bns (7, 308, 427, 551/651, 553, 559, 637 & 675) retreated with the Germans into Belarus, Poland, and finally Germany. Starting in Oct 1943, 21 bns (439, 441, 561, 600, 602, 605, 615, 618, 621, 627, 629, 630, 633–636, 642, 643, 649, 680 & 752) transferred to the 7th and 15th Armies in northern France (including 643rd Bn on Jersey, Channel Islands), and would suffer heavy casualties after the Normandy landings of June 1944; and the 628th Bn fought in Belgium. Another 10 bns (406, 550, 601, 654, 661, 663, 665, 666, 669 & 681) served in southern France, mostly with 19th Army, opposing the Allied landings in Aug 1944. Meanwhile, 9 bns (263, 339, 412, 555, 556, 560, 616, 617 & 620) served in northern Italy, mainly with 10th Army. The 5 bns (603, 653, 662, 667 & 674) based in Denmark under 166th Reserve and 416 Inf Divs formed, in Apr 1945, 599th Russian Bde, including 1607th Eastern Legion Regiment.

The Volunteer Depot Division *(Freiwilligen-Stamm-Division)* was formed on 1 Feb 1944 in Castres, southern France, to train ROA, Eastern Legion and Cossack recruits in 1st–5th Regiments. Its 4th Regt, formed on 7 March 1944 from the Eastern Replacement Regt, trained Russians and Ukrainians, but Russians only from June 1944. Eastern Regt HQ 752 was reorganized in Apr 1944 as a Special Purpose Gren Regt *(Grenadier-Regt zb V)*,

On 19 April 1944, Eastern Bn 643 transferred to Jersey in the Channel Islands as IV Bn/Static *(bodenständig)* Gren Regt 582, part of 319th Grenadier Division. Here a company march through the countryside wearing mostly M1944 uniforms and insignia; they are almost indistinguishable from German troops apart from the ROA red-blue oval badges high on the front of their M1942 field caps. (Courtesy, Central Museum of the Armed Forces, Moscow, via Stavka)

with infantry, 752nd Eastern Arty Bn and 752nd Eastern Eng Co, but was destroyed in Normandy. In France, Italy and Denmark 24 bns were taken into German reserve, grenadier and fortress grenadier regts, but from June 1944 some regained their identities as 'Russian' or 'Ukrainian' units.

Uniforms and insignia

Regulation 32003/44 of 18 March 1944 allowed 'suitable' ROA personnel and Hilfswillige to adopt German collar patches, branch pipings and rank insignia with Russian rank titles for NCOs and men, and from 15 April 1944 the eagle-and-swastika on the tunic breast and headgear. The M1943 oval cap badge, and for Eastern Bns the ROA arm shield, were still worn, and 'unsuitable' personnel retained their M1943 insignia. All ranks up to general were theoretically open to the Volunteers. Germans who qualified as Russian interpreters wore a white or crimson armband on the left upper sleeve with 'Wehrmacht/Dolmetscher' (Armed Forces Interpreter) in two lines of black print, and an official stamp. Russians with a basic knowledge of German wore a black cloth sleeve-band on the left cuff with 'Sprachmittler' (language mediator, or 'go-between') in white.

Russian People's Liberation Committee (KONR) and Armed Forces (VS-KONR), 1944–45

On 16 Sept 1944, Reichsführer-SS Heinrich Himmler, commanding the German Replacement Army comprising all troops in Germany, promoted Vlasov to full general and authorized the formation of 45,000 Russians into three infantry divisions. On 14 Nov 1944 Vlasov established the Russian People's Liberation Committee (*Komitet Osvobozheniya Narodov Rossii* – KONR) in German-occupied Prague, advocating in his 'Prague Manifesto' a democratic Russia allied to Germany. The KONR Armed Forces (*Vooruzhennye Sily KONR* – VS-KONR) were established, with Vlasov as C-in-C from 28 Jan 1945. Now at last he had some Russian troops under his operational control, although still under German strategic command.

The KONR troops wore German uniforms with German or M1943 ROA collar and rank insignia, and the ROA arm shield now on the right

General **Vlasov announces the KONR Manifesto in German-occupied Prague, 14 Nov 1944. (Seated, front row, left to right):** ***General-mayor*** **Fedor I. Trukhin, chief of staff;** ***General-leytenant*** **Georgiy N. Zhilenkov, head of the Propaganda Dept; Vlasov. (Standing behind, left to right, wearing adjutant's aiguillettes):** ***Polkovnik*** **Vladimir V. Pozdnyakov, and** ***Polkovnik*** **Igor K. Sacharov. Vlasov wears his M1943 uniform, Trukhin and Zhilenkov German generals' uniforms, and Pozdnyakov German field officers' uniform, all three with the M1943 ROA arm shield now shifted to the right sleeve for KONR troops. Sacharov wears an M1943 ROA uniform. (Tchakov Collection)**

Table 2: Russian Liberation Army formations & major units, 24 Aug 1941–8 May 1945

VS-KONR:

- *600 (Russian) Inf Div, aka 1st Div* (r. 10.11.1944, W. Germany); 4.1945, E. Germany; 5.1945, Prague. *Component units:*– Gren Regts 1601–1603 (each I, II Bns); 10.3.1945, 1604 Gren Regt; Arty Regt 1600 (I–IV Bns); AT Bn 1600; support services numbered 1600
- *650 (Russian) Inf Div, aka 2nd Div* (r. 3.1945, W. Germany) – Gren Regts 1651–1653 (each I, II Bns); Arty Regt 1650 (I–IV Bns); support services numbered 1650
- *700 (Russian) Inf Div, aka 3rd Div* (r. 4.1945, W. Germany) – Div HQ and recruits only
- *Russian Anti-Tank Bde* (r. 1.2.1945, W. Germany) – (Russian) AT Units 10 & 11, E. Germany; 8.3.1945, (Russian) AT Units 13 & 14, E. Germany
- *(Russian) Training & Replacement Bde, aka Reserve Bde* (r. 2.1945) – 1 Regt; Arty, Mot, Sigs, Eng, Ordnance Bns; Mtd Sqn

Russian Liberation Army major units & headquarters (not part of VS-KONR):

- *Tietjen Intervention Group* (r. 24.8.1941, C. Russia) – 1–6 Russian Cos, became I–III/582 Volunteer Bns, etc.; 1.11.1942, Staff Officer Eastern Troops 582; 28.1.43, OC Eastern Troops 709, C. Russia; 31.8.1943, disbanded
- *Hohlfeld Special HQ* (r. 27.1.1942, C. Russia) – Eastern Combat Bns Beresina, Dnjepr, Düna, Pripjet & Wolga; 15.7.1942, Eastern Replacement Regt, Army Group Centre; 19.1.1943, OC Eastern Troops 701; 12.1943, Eastern Training Regt, Army Group Centre; 4.1944, disbanded
- *Volunteer Regt 'Weise'* (r. 1.7.1942, C. Russia) – I, II & Arty Training Bns; 5.10.1942, Volunteer Regt 'Dessna' (I–III Bns); 18.11.1942, Eastern Bns 615–617
- *Anti-Partisan Light Bn* (r. summer 1942, N. Russia); 2.10.1942, Irregular Light Regt 16 – I–III Bns; 14.1.1943 – Eastern Bns 667–669
- *Eastern Staff, 532 Rear Area* (r. 11.1942, C. Russia); 1.2.1943, OC Eastern Troops 702 (Vol Bns); 2.10.43, S. France; 28.2.1944, disbanded
- *OC Eastern Troops 700* (r. 15.11.1942, C. Russia) – Eastern Bns 633–637; 11.1943, N. France; 2.1944, Eastern Regt HQ 752; 4.1944, Special Gren Regt 752, N. France (incl. Eastern Arty Bn 752); 6. 1944, destroyed, N. France
- *OC Eastern Troops 710* (r. 10.12.1942, N. Russia); 9.4.1943, Findeisen Regt HQ; 12.8.1943, Klobe Regt HQ; 12.9.1943, Eastern Regt HQ 753
- *Eastern Replacement Bn 4* (r. winter 1942, C. Russia); 6.12.1943, Eastern Replacement Regt; 12.6.1944, (Russian) Vol Depot Regt 4, France; 1945, Convalescent Bn/272 Inf Div, W. Germany
- *OC Eastern Troops 720* (r. early 1943, S. Russia); 12.1943, disbanded
- *OC Eastern Troops 721* (r. early 1943, S. Russia); 10.1943, N. France; 5.1944, 136 Inf Div HQ
- *OC Eastern Troops 703* (r. 1.2.1943, C. Russia) – Cossack Bns 622–625; 10.1943, Eastern Regt HQ, N. France; 18.5.1944, Commander Vol Units, Western Command, France
- *OC Eastern Troops 704* (r. 1.2.1943, C. Russia); 12.1943, disbanded
- *OC Eastern Troops 711* (r. 4.1943, N. Russia): Welcker Eastern Bn; 8.12.1943, Eastern Training Regt, Army Group Centre, Belarus; 4.1944, disbanded
- *OC Eastern Troops 741* (r. 20.5.1943, S. Russia); 1943, disbanded
- *OC Eastern Troops 712* (r. 1.9.1943, N. Russia); probably not formed
- *Eastern Regt HQ 755* (r. 12.9.1943, C. Russia); 1944?, disbanded
- *Eastern Regt HQ 751* (r. 10.1943, S. France); 2.1944, Eastern Bn 561
- *OC Eastern Troops Generalgouvernement* (r. 15.2.1944); 30.9.1944, disbanded
- *(Eastern) Gren Regt 714* (r. 30.4.1944, Denmark); 22.6.1944, (Russian) Gren Regt 714, Denmark; 3.1945, (Russian) Gren Regt 1604
- *Eastern Regt HQ 580* (r. 1944?); probably not formed
- *Russian Bde 599* (r. 3.1945, Denmark) – (Russian) Gren Regts 1604, 1605, 1607 (each I–III Bns), Arty Regt 1599

upper sleeve; they removed the eagle-and-swastika cap and breast badges from 2 March 1945. German cadre personnel retained the eagle-and-swastika but removed the ROA arm shield. Hiwis and Eastern Bns, including 599th Russian Bde in Denmark, remained beyond Vlasov's grasp; they retained the eagle-and-swastika, and the ROA arm shield on the left sleeve.

The VS-KONR comprised an HQ; eventually, three infantry divisions; a 7,000-man Training & Replacement Bde (including a Soviet T-34 tank company), providing enlisted replacements for the ROA divisions, and the 1,242-strong Anti-Tank Bde-Russian *(Panzerjägerbrigade R)*, both of the latter being formed in Feb 1945; and an Officers' Academy at Dabendorf, near Berlin. (The Academy had originally been formed on 1 March 1943, its true purpose being disguised by sympathetic German officers as the 'Eastern Propaganda Detachment for Special Purposes'.)

The AT Brigade-Russian comprised four 310-man groups, each of three units, each divided into ten sections. Its 10th Unit fought in the German AT Div Weichsel on the Oder Front in Feb 1945, followed by 11th Unit in March.

The three infantry divisions, under KONR chief-of-staff GenMay Fedor I. Trukhin, were formed in Württemberg, south-west Germany from new POW volunteers on a nucleus of 13 Eastern Bns (308, 427,

600, 601, 605, 618, 628, 630, 663, 666, 675, 681 & 752) from France. Each division had three 2-bn infantry regts, a 4-bn artillery regt and supporting services, but the 22,000-strong 1st KONR Div (numbered 600th Div in the German battle-order) also had an AT bn with 10 Jagdpanzer 38(t) self-propelled guns and some T-34 tanks. The 1st Div began forming in Nov 1944 at Münsingen, and was operational in March 1945, but the 2nd Div (650th) and the 10,000-strong 3rd Div (700th) were still training at Heuberg in May 1945.

On 6 March 1945 the 1st Div, under GenMay Sergey K. Bunyachenko, left Münsingen and reported on 4 Apr to German 9th Army, Army Group Weichsel (Vistula) on the Oder Front. Meanwhile, 599th Russian Bde was dispersed in Feb 1945, with 1604th Regt fighting on the Oder Front at Gartz south of Stettin on 10 March under 3rd Pz Army, and transferring to 1st KONR Div on 9 April. The 1st Div attacked the Soviet 33rd Army bridgehead at Erlenhof near Fürstenberg on 13 Apr, but after initial success was forced back.

Ignoring German orders, Bunyachenko retreated southwards, reaching Prague; there he supported the Czech National Council's seizure of the city on 6–7 May by capturing the airport and main railway station from the German garrison. The following day he retreated westwards before the approaching Red Army, and surrendered to Gen Patton's US 3rd Army at Lnáře on 10 May.

Meanwhile, on 19 Apr, 25,000 men of the KONR HQ, 2nd Div (GenMay G.A. Zverev), 3rd Div (GenMay Mikhail M. Shapovalov), Reserve Bde and Officers' Academy left Münsingen and Heuberg, reaching Linz on 1 May and surrendering to Patton at České Budějovice on 9 May. The demoralized Gen Vlasov played no part in directing these operations.

Following a secret codicil of 31 March 1945 to the Yalta Agreement of 11 Feb, British and US forces repatriated all Russian POWs to the Soviet Union. On 2 Aug 1946, 12 KONR generals, including Vlasov, Zhilenkov, Trukhin, Bunyachenko and Zverev, were hanged in Moscow. Other KONR troops were either shot, or imprisoned in Gulag concentration camps, which many did not survive.

The Eastern *Luftwaffe*

Hiwis served in all types of Luftwaffe units, wearing German or Soviet uniforms with M1941 armbands. In Oct 1943 Luftwaffe Obstlt Walter Holters recruited Red Army Air Force prisoners into *Fliegergruppe Holters*, to repair and service captured Soviet aircraft. That December the 1st Eastern Flying Sqn (Russian) – *1. Ostfliegerstaffel (russische)* – was formed at Daugavpils, Latvia, flying Arado Ar 66, Gotha Go 145, Polikarpov Po-2 and Yakovlev UT-2 armed trainers on night intruder missions until July 1944. From 1942, Russian aircrews were routinely flying in Luftwaffe units, including a Light Anti-Partisan Sqn equipped with 9x Po-2s in Belarus. From 29 May 1943 these personnel wore M1943 ROA cap cockades, collar patches, grey-blue shoulder straps (highest rank *Polkovnik*, Col), and M1943 ROA arm shields on a grey-blue background on the left sleeve.

On 19 Dec 1944 the 7,500-strong KONR Air Force (*Voyenno-Vozdushnye Sily KONR* – VVS-KONR) was formed by Polkovnik (12 Feb 1945, GenMay) Viktor I. Mal'cev. The 1st Flying Regt, formed 10 Feb 1945 at Eger (now Cheb, Czech Republic), comprised 7 sqns: 3rd Recce; 4th Transport

(Junkers Ju 52); 5th 'Colonel Kazakov' Fighter (Messerschmitt Bf 109G-10); 8th Ground Attack, redesignated 28 Mar 1945 as Night Intruder (12x Junkers Ju 88); 11th Bomber; 14th Liaison; and 5th Training (10 assorted aircraft). Only 5th and 8th Sqns were ever combat-ready, and 8th Sqn saw action supporting 1st KONR Div at the Erlenhof bridgehead on 13 April. Non-flying personnel, including the 2,800-strong 9th AA Regt, Air Sigs units and 9th Parachute Bn, were converted to infantry in late March 1945. (Mal'cev was hanged in Moscow in Aug 1946.)

Three ROA officers serving in the Luftwaffe's anti-aircraft artillery, autumn 1944. All wear M1935 grey-blue service uniforms with red branch-colour collar patches and shoulder-strap underlay. The *Podporuchik* (left) has an M1943 ROA arm shield on the right sleeve, the *Poruchik* (centre) likewise on the left sleeve, and all three officers have the Iron Cross 2nd Class buttonhole-ribbon. Eastern personnel were eligible for the Luftwaffe's M1941 Flak War Badge. (Tchakov Collection)

Following Regulation 32003/44 of 18 March 1944, the VVS-KONR wore standard M1935 grey-blue Luftwaffe uniforms complete with collar, shoulder-strap and sleeve rank insignia and eagle-and-swastika badges, and the M1943 ROA shield on the right upper sleeve. The eagle-and-swastika was worn on the peaked service cap above a red-blue-silver oval cockade within a Luftwaffe wreath with stylized wings. Later the winged wreath was removed, followed on 2 March 1945 by the cap and breast-eagles, although many personnel simply cut off the swastika.

From March 1944, Russian youths aged 15–20 manned AA batteries as Eastern Peoples' Air Force Auxiliaries *(Luftwaffenhelfer der Ostvölker)*. They wore a blue-grey Hitler Youth (*Hitlerjugend* – HJ) uniform comprising an M1943 peaked cap with a diamond-shaped cloth badge horizontally striped in white-blue-red; and a battledress blouse with black pointed shoulder straps piped light blue, with HJ rank insignia. They wore on the left upper sleeve a white-blue-red horizontally striped armband with a St Andrew's Cross in blue on a white shield, on a white diamond piped red. In Dec 1944 the 1,383 remaining youths were redesignated SS-Cadets (sing. *SS-Zögling*), adding above the left armband white SS runes on a black cloth triangle with a white inner border. From summer 1944 several thousand women served as Eastern AA Combat Female Auxiliaries *(Flakkampfhelferinnen Ost)*, wearing M1943 blue-grey field caps and tunics, with the St Andrew's Cross shield on a diagonally striped diamond on the left upper sleeve.

INDEPENDENT RUSSIAN VOLUNTEER UNITS

Four organizations were formed by charismatic anti-Communist or émigré Russians or Germans from the Baltic States, supported by Army High Command (*Oberkommando des Heeres* – OKH) and Army Intelligence *(Abwehr)*, the latter being absorbed from 18 Jan 1944 by SS Intelligence (*Sicherheitsdienst* – SD). Unlike the situation in the ROA, Russian officers occupied most command positions. These units played a significant role on the Eastern Front, but never attained the scale or success of the Eastern Bns and Cossacks.

These RNNA officers in 1943 wear Soviet uniform with mixed badges: M1935 *pilotka* field caps with M1942 RNNA cockades (2nd left has a smaller variant); M1935 field shirts with fly fronts (2nd right has the M1929 pattern with visible front buttons); and Red Army M1935 red parallelogram service-dress collar patches piped black. They wear non-regulation shoulder straps: the *starshiy leytenant* at 2nd right has field officers' lengthways stripes, the others plain or ROA shoulder straps. Note the M1932 leather belts with single cross-braces. (Tchakov Collection)

Russian Nationalist People's Army (RNNA)

In March 1942 a Russian anti-Communist, Sergei N. Ivanov (codename *Graukopf* – 'Grey Head'), then serving as a Sonderführer with AG Centre, persuaded the Abwehr to form about 150 Russian POWs at Osintorf (now Osinovka), near Smolensk in Belarus, into a recce and sabotage unit for missions behind Soviet lines. However, the inability of the Luftwaffe's special operations unit KG 200 to allocate aircraft prevented such clandestine insertions, and the men were diverted to anti-partisan operations. The unit was known successively as Abwehr Detachment *(Abwehrabteilung)* 203; 'Grey Head' Special Unit *(Sonderverband Graukopf)*; Special Russian Bn *(Rußisches Bataillon zb V)*; and finally Experimental Unit, Centre *(Versuchsverband Mitte)*. The German liaison officers and commanders were Abwehr officers, the personnel Russian émigrés or prisoners of war. The nominal Russian commanders were Pukovnik Konstantin G. Kromiadi, from 1 Sept 1942 Pukovnik Vladimir Boyarsky, and finally Pukovnik Ril; the political officer was Polkovnik Georgiy N. Zhilenkov.

These men, who regarded themselves as the nucleus of a Russian anti-Communist army, defiantly named themselves the Russian Nationalist People's Army (*Russkaya Natsional'naya Narodnaya Armiya* – RNNA). By Dec 1942 it had 7,000 men in 5 infantry Experimental Bns *(Versuchsbataillone 1–5)*, 1 artillery and 1 engineer bn, and from Aug 1942 an Air Force training sqn (without aircraft) under Mayor Filatov. The RNNA fought Red Army stragglers and partisans in double-company actions in AG Centre's Rear Area with varying degrees of success – sometimes driving back the enemy and attracting deserters to its ranks, sometimes suffering defeats and desertions itself. Even its most successful engagement, by a 300-man detachment at Yelnia near Smolensk in May 1942 against an element of 1st Gds Cav Corps, was only a partial victory.

By Sept 1942 the RNNA had expanded to form a 7,000-strong brigade, called by the Germans the Boyarsky Bde or Osintorf Brigade. In Oct 1942 the sceptical commander of AG Centre, Generalfeldmarschall Günther von Kluge, closed down Operation 'Graukopf'; on 1 Nov he reorganized the brigade's *Versuchsbataillone* into *Ost-Bataillone* 633–637, under OC Eastern Troops 700, and issued all personnel with German uniforms. Some 600 men immediately deserted, forcing the Germans to redeploy the remainder in Rear Areas. Trapped between Russian ambition and German suspicions, the RNNA was disbanded in Feb 1943.

The RNNA personnel wore Red Army khaki uniform with M1942 RNNA insignia. Headgear comprised the M1935 officers' peaked cap with red crown piping and band, and a distinctive red (inner)-blue-silver cockade; the M1935 officers' *pilotka* field cap (officers with gold flap and crown piping) with cockade; and the M1940 helmet. The M1929 or M1935 officers' field shirt had red collar- and cuff-piping, and M1942 shoulder straps piped red with gold lengthways stripes and M1924 enamel rank bars or squares edged yellow. The M1935 rhomboid-shape ceremonial and parallelogram-shape service-dress collar patches were piped gold or black. Officers wore the M1932 leather belt and cross-brace, M1935 royal-blue *sharovary* breeches with red piping, and black riding boots. Enlisted men wore field shirts without piping or collar patches, M1924 red enamel rank triangles edged yellow on plain shoulder straps, M1912 belts, khaki trousers, and black marching boots.

This RNNA *mladshiy serzhant* in 1942 wears the M1935 *pilotka* field cap without red piping, and the M1942 RNNA cockade. His field shirt has no collar patches; the M1942 RNNA shoulder straps are unpiped, but bear a red enamel rank triangle edged yellow. (Tchakov Collection)

SS-Verband Drushina

In March 1942 the SD began recruiting Russian POWs into a battalion-sized SS Unit Drushina *(SS-Verband Drushina)*, for Operation 'Zeppelin' missions behind Soviet lines, but, like the RNNA's Operation 'Graukopf', from May 1942 it was diverted to anti-partisan work. 'Drushina' *(druzhina)* was the historic term for a medieval Russian prince's bodyguard. In Apr 1942, Drushina I was formed under Mayor Vladimir V. Gil with 500 men. German SD cadre personnel wore M1937 'SD' uniforms – actually Waffen-SS uniforms and insignia with blank right collar patches, and the 'SD' diamond badge on the left forearm. Russians wore a red-blue-silver cockade on the sidecap, but no 'SD' diamond. A black cuff-band edged in silver-grey thread, with *Za Rus* ('for Russia') in Church Slavonic script, may have been worn on the left sleeve.

Initially the unit fought well against Belarusian partisans, but from late 1942 morale deteriorated. On 11 Dec 1942, Drushina II was formed under Mayor Andrey Blazhevich with only 135 men, and in March 1943 both units were combined as the 1,350-strong Drushina SS-Regt (to the Russians,1st Russian National SS Regt), with an HQ and Infantry Bns I–IV. In May 1943 this was reorganized as the Drushina SS-Bde (1st

Two officers of the 1st ROA Guards Bde at a parade in Pskov, 22 June 1943, the second anniversary of the German invasion of the USSR. Although formerly from the SS-Drushina Unit, they still wear some insignia from the disbanded RNNA. *Podpolkovnik* Igor K. Sacharov (right) wears an RNNA officers' peaked cap with M1943 ROA cockade; a white Tsarist summer field shirt with standing collar, M1943 ROA shoulder straps with white lengthways stripes, an M1943 ROA shield on his left upper arm, and a German black Wound Badge. His companion wears a turn-down collar with M1943 RNNA red rhomboid collar patches piped gold. (Tchakov Collection)

Russian National SS Bde), with 3,000 men in I–III Infantry and I
Training and Artillery Bns, transport and MG cos, and an AA bty; it wa
commanded by Polkovnik Gil, but he now called himself 'Rodionov'.

In May 1943, ROA GenLt Zhilenkov informed Rodionov that Drushin
would join the ROA as 1st ROA Guards Brigade. Unwilling to lose hi
independence, Rodionov bought time by redesignating IV Training B
as I Bn, 1st ROA Guards Brigade. The unit paraded at Pskov, wester
Russia on 22 June 1943, and participated in anti-partisan operation
Meanwhile, Rodionov contacted the Soviet Zhelezniak Partisan Bde t
arrange his defection, and on 13 Aug 1943 he and 400 men of I B
crossed to Soviet lines; they formed the 1st Anti-Fascist Partisan Bd
which was destroyed in Apr 1944. The remaining 30 officers and 500 me
of I Bn regained German lines, where they were absorbed into the 1s
ROA Guards Bde at Pskov under former RNNA officer Pukovnik Serg
Ivanov, only to be disbanded in Nov 1943; II–IV Bns had been disbande
on 23 Aug 1943.

Russian People's Liberation Army (RONA)

On 6 Oct 1941, 2nd Pz Army occupied Lokot in the Bryansk region o
western Russia. This fell under Korück 532's authority, and in Novembe
that command appointed Konstantin P. Voskobojnik as mayor of Loko
SVB. Voskobojnik established a 300-strong People's Police *(Narodn
Militsiya)*, wearing white armbands with a black St George's (i.e. Maltese
Cross; this force kept order, guarded the Bryansk–Lygev railway, an
fought partisans. By Jan 1942 it had 500 men, but Voskobojnik was kille
in action on 8 Jan 1942. The Polish-German engineer Bronisław V
Kaminski then became mayor, and by spring 1942 he had 1,200 policeme
fighting alongside German and Hungarian forces.

On 19 July 1942, Kaminski reorganized his police into a 10,000-stron
People's Defence Bde *(Volksheerbrigade)*, wearing German and Red Arm
uniforms or civilian clothes. By Feb 1943 this had an HQ (with Eng, Sig
and Medical cos); a Guards Bn; and 15 infantry bns numbered I–XV
each defending a geographical area and distributed sequentially betwee

August 1944: officers of the RONA Special Regt in Warsaw, scene of the 'Kaminski Brigade's' most infamous atrocities. Three of them wear plain *kubanka* caps. (Far left) has a German M1935 officers' tunic with M1940 collar patches and breast-eagle. Next to him (2nd left) is a German Schutzpolizei officer. (Centre) is *Waffen-Stubaf* Ivan D. Frolov, OC the Special Regt; he wears a German M1940 tunic and collar patches, but Cossack M1943 silver service-dress shoulder straps with red piping and centre-stripes, blue *sharovary* breeches, and riding boots. *Podporuchik* Michalczewski (2nd right) wears royal-blue *sharovary.* (Far right) is an ROA tank officer, commanding an attached troop of four T-34s; he wears a German M1943 field-grey field cap and M1942 Panzer troops' black uniform, with M1935 skull collar patches piped pink, German subaltern officers' shoulder straps with pink underlay (permitted from 18 March 1944), and an M1943 ROA arm shield. (Archive of Party History, Record A-3798, 1944)

1st–5th Inf Regts; a 36-gun artillery bn, and an armoured bn with 24x T-34 tanks. By May 1943 Kaminski, promoted to *Brigadekommandeur*, had reformed the People's Defence Bde as the Russian People's Liberation Army (*Russkaya Osvoboditelnaya Narodnaya Armiya* – RONA). Personnel wore M1943 ROA uniforms and insignia, with a dark bluish-green arm shield with a gold 'POHA' – the Cyrillic form of RONA – above a white shield edged black and bearing a black St George's Cross (though it was manufactured in several variant forms).

Kaminski responded to partisan activity with conscription and atrocities against civilians, and as a consequence RONA suffered sinking morale and increasing desertions. In Aug 1943, reduced to about 6,000 men, it retreated with its civilian dependants to form a new SVB at Lepel, northern Belarus, under Korück 590. From Jan 1944 Kaminski defended Lepel SVB against the partisans, but in May they retreated again to Lida in central Belarus, with 4,000 soldiers in 1st–3rd Regts and 21,000 civilians.

In June 1944 RONA was transferred to the Waffen-SS at Częstochowa in the Polish Generalgouvernement, as the non-Germanic Assault Brigade RONA *(Waffen-Sturm-Brigade RONA)*, with Kaminski ranking as a *Waffen-Brigadeführer der SS*, although no personnel wore Waffen-SS uniforms or insignia. In July 1944 the bde transferred to Neuhammer (now Świętoszów, Poland), but plans to form from it a 29. *Waffen-Grenadier-Division der SS (russische Nr. 1)* on 1 Aug 1944 were overtaken by the Warsaw Uprising. A 1,585-strong Special Regt under *Waffen-Sturmbannführer* Ivan D. Frolov, with 2 infantry bns, artillery, a tank and a self-propelled gun, fought the rising from 4–27 August. They murdered up to 10,000 civilians in the 'Ochota Massacre', which prompted the SS to execute Kaminski near Łódź on 28 Aug 1944. The bde, under Podpolkovnik Belay, fought against the Slovak National Uprising in Sept 1944 before its disbandment in October. The men were reluctantly accepted into the 1602nd Regt of KONR's 1st Div at Münsingen in Nov 1944, fighting on the Oder Front in March 1945. Thus ended what was the most disastrous example of German recruitment policy in Russia.

1st Russian National Army (1-ya RNA)

A Russian émigré intelligence expert, Count Boris A. Smyslovsky, commanded the Eastern Bn of the Russian All-Military Union (*Russkij Obsche-Voinskij Soyuz* – ROVS) based in Warsaw, and in July 1941, serving as 'Maj Regenau', he formed an Abwehr Training Bn *(Lehrbataillon)* for recce and anti-partisan duties under AG North. By Dec 1942 Smyslovsky had recruited 10,000 Red Army deserters and POWs into 12 recce bns, later unified as the 1001st Gren Regt within Special Div–Russia *(Sonderdivision R)*. Standard ROA uniforms and insignia were introduced on 29 May 1943. Meanwhile, in March 1942, Smyslovsky formed the Special HQ–Russia *(Sonderstab R)* counter-intelligence agency in Warsaw, with Col Mikhail M. Shapovalov controlling 1,000 agents in detachments in Pskov, Minsk, Kiev and Simferopol, gathering intelligence on partisans in the Rear Areas.

Smyslovsky was trusted by the German Army but not by the SS, who were suspicious of his links with Polish Home Army (*Armia Krajowa* – AK) and Ukrainian Insurgent Army (*Ukrains'ka Povstans'ka Armiya* – UPA) guerrillas. In Dec 1943 the SD disbanded the Special HQ-R and Div-R and arrested Smyslovsky. In June 1944 he was declared innocent, and the

Special Div was immediately reinstated in Breslau (now Wrocław, Poland). Special Div personnel wore German uniforms, rank and other insignia, with a Russian arm shield on the left upper sleeve, and used M1944 ROA Russian rank titles. While it was still forming, the 4-regt Special Div was evacuated in Jan 1945 to Bad Elster, Saxony; and on 12 Feb it was codenamed Special Green Army *(Grüne Armee zb V)*, with 6,000 men. On 4 Apr 1945 the organization was renamed yet again, as 1st Russian National Army (*1-ya Russkaya Natsional'naya Armiya* – 1-ya RNA) under GenMaj Smyslovsky, with an HQ and 1st and 2nd Inf Regts with mostly Russian commanders.

On 18 Apr 1945 Smyslovsky, now calling himself 'Arthur Holmston', refused Vlasov's offer to join the KONR and began retreating westwards with his remaining 462 men. On 2 May they removed their German cap- and breast-eagles and Smyslovsky his general's collar patches, and crossed from Feldkirch, Austria, to internment in neutral Liechtenstein. From there about 200 personnel voluntarily returned to the USSR; the remainder emigrated to Argentina in 1947. Smyslovsky died in Vaduz, Liechtenstein in 1988.

RUSSIAN COSSACKS

Origins

Communities of Russian Cossacks emerged in the 16th century, each organized in a 'host' *(Voysko)*, and were allotted farming land in buffer zones on the southern borderlands of the Russian Empire, where they confronted Turkic and Tartar forces. Cossacks soon established a reputation for horsemanship and bravery, but also for an independent spirit which sometimes conflicted with their loyalty to the Tsars. By the late 18th century Cossacks had become a distinct military caste, often employed to suppress rebellions. By Aug 1914 there were 13 Russian Cossack hosts, each named after a city or river within their territory. The 6 European hosts were the Don (lower Don Basin), Kuban and Terek (Caucasus), and the Astrakhan, Ural and Orenburg (Urals); the 7 Asian hosts were the Siberian, Semirechen and Transbaikal (Siberia), and the Amur, Ussuri, Yenisei and Irkutsk (Far East). The Zaporozhian Cossacks were Ukrainians.

Cossacks fought on both sides in the Russian Civil War (1918–22) but featured more prominently in the White Armies, when the Don, Kuban and Terek hosts enjoyed brief political independence. Inevitably, the Soviet government persecuted the Cossacks thereafter, but from 20 Apr 1936 they recruited Don, Kuban and Terek regts into the Red Army. During World War II they formed 17 Red Army cavalry corps, but a substantial number also joined the German Army.

A Kuban Cossack poses between a German military policeman and a tall German officer, 1942. The Cossack wears a plain black *kubanka* cap; a red *beshmet* field shirt; and a black *cherkeska* coat with red cuffs, and two sets of six cartridge-tubes with white ornamental caps. He wears a decorated *pojas* belt with a privately purchased *kindzhal* dagger in a silver sheath, and a strap for his *shashqa* sword over his right shoulder. He has a red *bashlyk* hood thrown back from his shoulders. For the elements of Cossack traditional dress, see also Plate E1. (Tchakov Collection)

By Dec 1941, AGs North and Centre had halted their advance in the face of increasingly effective Soviet opposition, but AG South held their gains in Ukraine during the winter. In July 1942 AG South formed two separate Army Groups, with 'A' occupying the Don lands of the Donets Basin and 'B' the Terek and Kuban lands of the north-western Caucasus. Cossacks had volunteered individually as Hiwis for the advancing German divisions from June 1941, and often deserted to them in entire company-strength mounted sqns (sing. *sotnia*; German, *Reiter-Hundertschaft*), mounted bns (sing. *divizion*; German, *Abteilung*), infantry bns (sing. *batal'on*; German, *Bataillon*), or regiments. There were also Cossack infantry, called *Plastun*.

Cossack Hiwis wore Soviet or German uniforms, civilian clothes, or traditional Cossack dress with royal-blue breeches. Don Cossacks had dark blue uniforms with red piping and facings, comprising a tall black lambswool *papacha* cap with a red cloth top or a dark blue peaked cap with red band, a high-collared tunic, and wide red breeches-stripes. Kuban and Terek Cossacks wore Caucasian dress. Kuban Cossacks had a low black lambswool *kubanka* cap with a red cloth top, red *beshmet* linen field shirt, brown or black *cherkeska* ankle-length coat, red *bashlyk* hood, red-piped breeches and a *pojas* belt with hanging straps. Terek Cossacks had a black *kubanka* with a cornflower-blue top, cornflower-blue *beshmet* and *bashlyk*, grey *cherkeska*, and cornflower-blue breeches-piping. Tsarist Russian *pogoni* shoulder straps were worn, and special pre-Revolutionary Cossack rank titles were used.

The deluded Hitler believed the Cossacks to be descendants of Germanic Goths, and thus quietly tolerated their recruitment at regimental strength, while the Cossacks' military prestige attracted many aristocratic German cavalry officers to serve as cadres.

Cossack Security units, June 1941–December 1942

The first Cossack units were designated Security Bns, while the mounted regts were intended for the planned 1st Cossack Division. By Dec 1942, 15 regts and 14 bns had been formed. Army Group North had 3 Cossack mtd sqns numbered 207, 281 & 285, later designated mtd battalions. Army Group Centre had 12th *Plastun* Regt and two Security bns numbered 137 & 600. On 22 Aug 1941, Red Army Podpolkovnik Ivan N. Kononov came over to the Germans with his 436th Rifle Regt (of 155th Rifle Div) at Mogilev, eastern Belarus, declaring his regiment's willingness to fight against Stalin. General Max von Schenckendorff, GOC AG Centre Rear Area, recognized Kononov's potential and, ignoring Hitler's orders, retained the regiment as 'Cossack Hundred 102', later Cossack Bn (*Kosaken-Abteilung*) 600. The 137th Mtd Bn was formed Oct 1942, and 4 sqns – 443 & 1–3/581 – became mtd bns in 1943.

A group of Cossacks from a Security Bn, summer 1942. The *Stellvertretender Zugführer* (right foreground) wears a stiffened Don Cossack lambswool cap; on the collar of his German M1935 field tunic a chevron of silver NCO braid edges the red Security unit collar patch, which bears two braid rank bars. His companions wear stiffened *papacha* or Caucasian *kubanka* caps, but only one (2nd left) shows the German eagle and cockade insignia. (Tchakov Collection)

Alexey Sovitshenko was a Don Cossack serving in a mounted battalion, mid-1943. He wears a *papacha* cap with a Tsarist officers' black-and-orange cockade with silver sunrays. His German M1935 tunic bears M1942 collar patches for his rank of trooper, but the shoulder straps of a *zauryad khorunzhiy*, suggesting that this former Soviet senior NCO is waiting for the Germans to promote him back to NCO rank. (Author's collection)

Between June and Dec 1942 the Don Cossack *Ataman* (host chieftain) Sergey Pavlov formed 14 mtd regts at the Cossack training centres at Shepetovka and Slavuta, central Ukraine, initially independent of German control: 1 Ataman, 2 Lifeguard, 3 Don, 4–5 Kuban, 6–8 Mixed (cav and inf), 9 Kuban, 10 Don, 11 Kuban, 12 Mixed, 14 Mixed & 1 Volga. Meanwhile, AG South had formed 3 mtd regts: Fürst von Urach/von Jungschultz, Pannwitz Mtd Unit, and Platov; and 8 Security bns (some originally sqns): 213, 299, 318, 403, 1/444, 2/444, 1/454 & 2/454. In early 1942, Maj Fürst Eberhard von Urach had formed a Cossack Mtd Bn, later under Obslt Werner Jungschultz von Roebern. The Pannwitz Mtd Unit *(Reiterverband von Pannwitz)*, under Obst Helmuth von Pannwitz, was a training unit for the planned Cossack Division.

In 1942 Alfred Rosenberg, Minister for Occupied Eastern Territories, established a Cossack Central Office *(Kosaken-Leitstelle)* in Berlin as part of his Eastern Ministry *(Ost-Ministerium)*. This office, redesignated Cossack Central Administration in March 1944, was headed by the German Dr Nikolai Himpel, succeeded on 25 Jan 1943 by the legendary 73-year-old Pyotr Krasnov – a Russian cavalry general, Don Cossack Ataman, and heroic leader of White forces in the Russian Civil War. Krasnov enlisted other distinguished ex-Civil War generals to tour POW camps and rear areas and encourage recruitment; notable among them were Gen Viacheslav G. Naumenko (Kuban Ataman), GenMay Simon N. Krasnov (Pyotr's great-nephew), and GenLt Andrei G. Shkuro.

Security unit uniforms and insignia, 1942

During 1942, Cossack units adopted German field-grey uniforms, and from June 1942 special insignia. German-issue headgear comprised the steel helmet without insignia; for officers, the M1938 officers' sidecap with silver-wire crown piping and red front flap piping; for NCOs and men, the M1934 enlisted ranks' sidecap with a white or red chevron point-up (officially abolished 10 July 1942), or the M1942 enlisted ranks' cap without piping, worn with an eagle-and-swastika above the German red-white-black national cockade, or without badges. Many Cossacks preferred the black lambswool *kubanka* or stiffened or unstiffened *papacha* caps with host-colour cloth tops, or royal-blue Tsarist-era peaked caps with host-colour crown piping and bands: red for Don and Kuban, cornflower-blue (mid-blue) for Terek. Cap insignia included Tsarist black-and-orange cockades, German M1935 matt silver Panzer collar skulls, Imperial German cavalry cap skulls, or the M1935 eagle and cockade. The M1935 service cap and M1934 officers' 'old style' field cap were reserved for German cadre officers and senior non-commissioned officers.

The German M1935 tunic with dark bluish-green collars and shoulder straps, or M1940, M1941 or M1943 tunics with field-grey collars and straps, initially had M1937 breast-eagles machine-woven in white on dark green backing, but from 1940 on field-grey; these were replaced in Aug 1942 by the M1942 'winged swastika' badge. Some units wore German Police tunics, including the M1936 Schutzpolizei or Gendarmerie service tunics with black or brown collars and cuffs respectively, or the M1942 or M1943 Schutzpolizei field-grey field tunics. The M1940, M1942 and M1943 pattern green or khaki tropical tunics were permitted for summer wear in Italy, southern France, the southern Balkans, Ukraine and the Caucasus. Some Cossacks were issued captured enemy uniform items especially the Royal Netherlands Army M1934 greyish-green tunic.

From 13 June 1942 the Platov (German, *Platow*) Regt prescribed bright red collar patches with silver-braid (usually German NCO) edging, rank bars and German four-pointed stars, and M1940 shoulder straps without piping. German positional titles were used. Officers wore braid collar edging and rank bars and stars, and white shoulder straps with 3–1 silver bars; NCOs and men wore collar-patch chevrons and rank bars, and 3–0 braid bars across bright red shoulder straps. M1935 medium grey or M1940 field-grey trousers were worn, often with Don Cossack red stripes, and M1939 short-shaft black leather marching boots, although field-grey and Russian royal-blue breeches and black riding boots were also worn. Three greatcoats were issued: the M1935 with a dark bluish-green collar and shoulder straps; the M1940 with field-grey collar and straps; and the M1942 with enlarged field-grey collar. Cossack officers wearing M1917 rank shoulder straps could retain them for personal prestige if they had not been awarded Security unit officer or NCO rank badges. German cadre personnel wore German uniforms and insignia.

Two Cossacks carry their wounded unit commander to a field dressing station, 1942. All are wearing M1940 field tunics with breeches or trousers and ankle boots. The troopers' *kubanka* caps show the Prussian cavalry skull-and-crossbones badge worn by the Von Jungschultz Cavalry Regt, while the commander has a Don Cossack *papacha* cap with a silvered German eagle badge. The *Reiter* on the left carries a Karabiner 98k rifle and a *naigaka* whip. (Author's collection)

Regulation 8000/42 of 20 Aug 1942 modified the Security unit rank insignia: Cossack officers now wore M1939 Sonderführer silver-wire shoulder straps, with modified silver-braid and star insignia on their collar patches; NCOs and men wore horizontal silver-braid rank bars (Zugführer, 2 vertical bars) on bright red rounded-end shoulder straps, and the June 1942 collar patches. The regulation of 11 Nov 1942 prescribed enlisted ranks' dark bluish-green shoulder straps and collar patches, the former with bright red piping.

Cossack units, December 1942–September 1943

By Dec 1942 Cossack forces were recognized as distinct from the Eastern Bns and Eastern Legions, although they carried the pejorative designation 'East'. They were heavily engaged against both partisans and the Red Army advancing into Belarus and Ukraine.

By Sept 1943, 14 Cossack regts and 16 bns could be identified. Army Group North had only 2 mtd bns: 281 & 285. AG Centre had 8 regts: Police Rifle 37, and 7 regts in the 1st Cossack Div – 1 Don, 2 Siberian, 3 & 4 Kuban, 5 Don & 6 Terek, supported by the Instruction & Training Regiment. Additionally there were 8 mtd bns: 213, 443, 580, 622, 623, 624, 625 & 631. In Ukraine, Pavlov had formed 5 regts: 1 Kuban, 1 Sinegorsk, 1 & 2 Volunteer Don, & Kuban *Plastun*. Army Group South had 454th Regt and 6 bns: 57, 161, 403, 570, 570 & 572. There were also

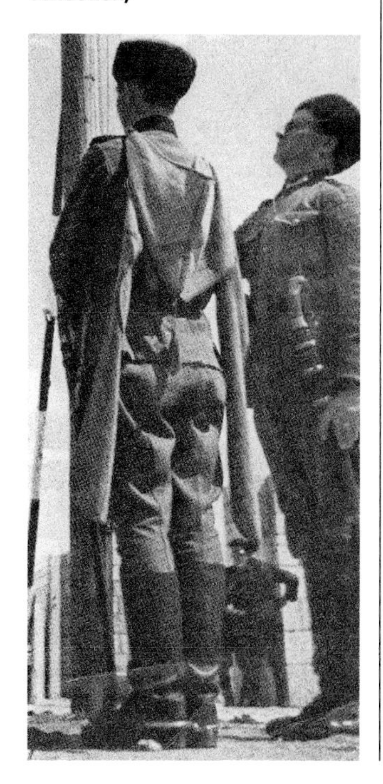

These Kuban Cossacks, hoisting a national flag in mid-1943, are wearing German M1935 tunics with M1940 enlisted ranks' collar patches, cavalry breeches, and riding boots with spurs. Note the 'sleeved' appearance of the thrown-back field-grey *bashlyk* hood with Kuban-red piping and tassel. Both men carry *shashqa* swords at their hips. (Author's collection)

This Don Cossack, resting with his horse in mid-1943, wears a *papacha* cap with a plain red cloth crown. His greenish-grey tunic is identifiable as a Royal Netherlands Army M1934 with seven front buttons and internal breast pockets, retailored with a turn-down collar. He displays the German M1940 breast-eagle and collar patches (instead of the regulation Cossack M1942 crossed-lances type); M1940 field-grey shoulder straps piped red, with Cossack *Unteroffizier* rank bars; and the 2nd-pattern Don host arm shield on his left upper sleeve. (Author's collection)

at least 19 company-sized Cossack units: 13 sqns, 2 *Plastun* cos, 1 arty bty and 3 construction companies.

Cossack uniforms and insignia, December 1942–May 1943

Regulation 10650/42 of 15 Nov 1942 (published 12 Dec) retained the officers' Sonderführer shoulder straps, but enlisted ranks' straps were now field-grey, with or without bright red piping. New collar patches were introduced, comprising silver-wire crossed lances on a bright red patch, edged in silver braid for officers and dark bluish-green cloth for NCOs and men. Non-commissioned officers ranking as *Stellvertretender Zugführer* and *Stellvertretender Gruppenführer* often wore German NCO silver-braid collar edging. Vertical white crossed lances against a vertical red bar were worn on a bluish-green oval patch on the sidecap, but Don Cossacks preferred a silver-braid cross on a red cloth oval edged dark blue. The Security units' M1942 'winged swastika' badge was worn on the right breast.

Round-based 'Spanish' shields with host insignia were introduced for the left upper sleeve, but multi-curved 'Polish' shields (with black cloth backing) were also worn unofficially. Patterns were either horizontal stripes or diagonal quarterings:

Don Cossacks: 1st pattern, yellow-blue-red stripes; 2nd, red (top/bottom) and blue (sides) quartering; 3rd, 'DON' above stripes.

Kuban Cossacks: 1st pattern, yellow and green quartering; 2nd, 'KUBAN' above quartering; 3rd, red and black quartering.

Terek Cossacks: 1st pattern, black-green-red stripes; 2nd, same with 'TEREK' above.

Cossack uniforms and insignia, May 1943–May 1945

Cossacks continued to wear German uniforms, including the peaked field cap introduced 11 June 1943, but not the M1944 battledress-style field blouse. They followed the Eastern Bns by adopting new field uniform insignia under Regulation Nr 141242/43 of 29 May 1943. All ranks wore two-coloured painted-metal oval cockades, officers having the outer oval shaped as sunrays: Don, red (inner) and blue; Kuban, red and black; Terek, blue and black.

This *Yesaul* of Terek Cossacks in 1943 sports complete German M1935 service-cap metal insignia (silver eagle-and-swastika, above black-white-red cockade within silver wreath) on his *kubanka* cap, which would have a cornflower-blue cloth crown. He has added pleats to his ex-Red Army khaki field shirt, and non-regulation German M1935 officers' silver-wire collar patches. His shoulder straps are Cossack M1943 service-dress quality, of silver braid with black piping, cornflower-blue centre-stripes, and two gilt German rank stars. The 4th-pattern Terek arm shield is visible on his left sleeve. (Tchakov Collection)

The M1943 ROA model dark green or field-grey field shoulder straps were introduced from 29 May 1943, but with special Cossack rank titles (no officer was promoted to general rank until Kononov, on 1 Apr 1945). To preserve the traditional host colours many Cossack officers wore M1943 silver- or gold-braid service-dress shoulder straps with German gold or silver four-point stars, coloured piping and centre

(Continued on page 3

RUSSIAN VOLUNTEER UNITS, 1941–42

1: *Hilfswilliger,* German 36th Mot Div; Kalinin, Oct 1941

2: *Kapitan,* RNNA; Osintorf, July 1942

3: *Kompanieführer,* 601st Beresina Eastern Bn; Bobruisk, Nov 1942

INDEPENDENT RUSSIAN VOLUNTEER UNITS, 1943–44
1: *Feldwebel,* 1st Inf Regt, Special Div R; Pruskow, Dec 1944
2: *Podporuchik,* Armd Bn, RONA; Lokot, Aug 1943
3: *Unteroffizier,* 1st Guards Bde, ROA; Pskov, June 1943

B

RUSSIAN LIBERATION ARMY, 1943–44
1: *GenLt* Georgiy N. Zhilenkov; Pskov, June 1943
2: Andrey A. Vlasov, Belarus, April 1943
3: *Fel'dfebel',* 635th Eastern Bn; Normandy, June 1944

C

KONR ARMED FORCES, 1945
1: *Ober-yefreytor, 1*601st Gren Regt; Erlenhof, April 1945
2: *Podporuchik,* 8th Night Intruder Sqn; Eger, March 1945
3: *Mayor,* 1603rd Gren Regt; Prague, May 1945

D

COSSACKS IN THE CAUCASUS CAMPAIGN, 1942–43
1: *Pod'esaul,* German 4th Mountain Div; Donetsk, March 1942
2: *Zugführer,* Platov Cossack Regt; Maikop, July 1942
3: *Stellvertretender Gruppenführer,* 7th Cossack Police Sqn, Feb 1943

E

COSSACK UNITS, 1943–44
1: ***Khorunzhiy,*** **360th Fortress Gren Regt; France, April 1944**
2: ***GenMaj*** **von Pannwitz, 1st Cossack Div; Croatia, Sept 1943**
3: ***Hauptwachtmeister,*** **11th Kuban Cossack Regt; Belarus, Sept 1943**

F

1st COSSACK DIVISION; CROATIA, 1943–44
1: *Unteroffizier,* Bodyguard Mtd Sqn; Fruška Gora, Oct 1943
2: *Oberleutnant,* 6th Terek Mtd Regt; Doboj, Nov 1943
3: *Sotnik,* II/55 Cossack Arty Bn; Prnjavor, Jan 1944

G

COSSACK CAVALRY CORPS; CROATIA, 1944–45
1: *Starshiy Prikasni,* 4th Kuban Mtd Regt; Valpovo, March 1945
2: *Polkovnik* I.N. Kononov, 5th Don Mtd Regt; Virovitica, Jan 1945
3: *Kazak,* 2nd Siberian Mtd Regt; Nova Gradiška, Sept 1944

H

Croatia, March 1944: *Voyskovoy starshina* Ivan Kononov (left), OC 5th Don Cossack Regt, with one of his bearded battalion commanders. Kononov wears a Don Cossack officers' unstiffened *papacha* cap with a German M1935 silver cap-eagle, above an M1942 Don Cossack red circular cockade with a silver-wire cross. His M1935 greatcoat has M1942 Cossack enlisted ranks' crossed-lances-on-red collar patches, commonly worn by officers on the dark bluish-green collar, and German field officers' plaited silver-cord shoulder straps on cavalry-yellow underlay. (For another of Kononov's uniforms, see Plate H2 opposite.) The *mayor* wears a lighter-coloured *papacha* with a woven silver eagle and German cockade on a T-shaped dark green backing, also above the Don Cossack cockade. His M1935 enlisted ranks' tunic has the same crossed-lances collar patches, German shoulder straps of rank, and a silver-wire breast-eagle. (Tchakov Collection)

stripes. Non-commissioned officers and men wore silver- or gold-braid bars and silver or gold metal stars on coloured, pointed shoulder straps with coloured piping:

Don Cossack officers: silver straps, red piping, dark blue centre-stripes; NCOs and men: dark blue straps piped red.

Kuban Cossack officers: silver straps, red piping and centre-stripes; NCOs and men: red straps piped red.

Terek Cossack officers: silver straps, black piping, cornflower-blue centre-stripes; NCOs and men: cornflower-blue straps piped black.

Artillery officers; gold straps, red piping, black centre-stripes; NCOs and men: black straps piped red.

Regulation 32003/44 of 18 March 1944 allowed Cossacks of proven military ability to wear German rank insignia (NCOs and men using Russian rank titles) and branch pipings (cavalry, golden-yellow; infantry, white; artillery, bright red). German collar patches could be worn (many tunics had been issued with these already sewn on), but the M1943 crossed-lances patches were widely retained. From 15 Apr 1944 the German breast-eagle could be worn.

22

An animated discussion between a Cossack and three members of the German cadre of his unit, probably Cossack Bn 624. His Red Army M1935 field shirt bears M1942 Cossack enlisted ranks' crossed-lances-on-red collar patches, and a 'winged' swastika right breast badge; he has the Soviet officers' brown leather belt equipment with two vertical braces, plus a cross-strap for his sword. The German *Feldwebel* (far right) wears the M1934 officers' 'old style' field cap; note on his left sleeve the red shield with three silver diagonal stripes (from top left) of Cossack Bn 624. (Author's collection)

***Major der Reserve* Uwe von Renteln commanded the Cossack Fortress Gren Regt 360 in the Charente-Maritime, south-west France, in March 1944. This cosmopolitan Baltic German, a veteran of the Tsar's Imperial Guard, would command the KONR 3rd Div's *Plastun* brigade in March 1945, and later tried (unsuccessfully) to negotiate with the British to avoid the repatriation of the Cossacks. On the M1935 service uniform he displays the M1943 ROA left-sleeve shield which replaced the regiment's former 'tank and F' badge (see Plate F1), and the silver-edged red shield, both worn by the regimental HQ. His ribbons are for the Iron Cross 2nd Class and Eastern Winter 1941/42 Medal; he also displays the pin-back Iron Cross 1st Class, a Wound Badge and the Tank Battle Badge. (Courtesy Central Museum of the Armed Forces, Moscow, via Stavka)**

Transfers to the West

In Feb 1943, following German 6th Army's collapse at Stalingrad, thousands of Don, Kuban and Terek civilian refugees trekked westwards into Ukraine and the Balkans, led by Ataman Pavlov and protected by his own Cossack units. In early 1943 they reached the Cossack Settlement *(Kazachi Stan)* provided for them by the Germans at Novogrudok (now Navahrudak), western Belarus. Meanwhile, 260 miles further west Obst Helmuth von Pannwitz was forming the 1st Cossack Div, formally established at Mława on 21 Apr 1943. This had 6 Cossack regts: Pannwitz Mtd Unit, 1, 1 Ataman, 1 Kuban, 1 Volga, and *Plastun* Inf; and 4 bns: 557, 558, 600, and *Plastun* 2 Battalion.

The Cossacks' prestige meant that relatively few Cossack units were transferred to other fronts after 10 Sept 1943. Two regts and 11 bns fought as infantry in France: 622nd and 623rd Cossack Bns formed Fortress Gren Regt 360, whilst 624th and 625th contributed battalions to Fortress Gren Regts 854 and 855 manning *Atlantikwall* bunkers on the south-west coast. Four bns, numbered 70 (ex-III/454), 403, II/454 & IV/454, were posted to the 5th Cossack Regt, Volunteer Depot Div at Castres, from where detachments defended the Atlantic Wall and fought the French Resistance. The 281st Bicycle Bn and 285th Mtd Bn fought in north-west France and were trapped in the Lorient pocket in May 1945, and 570th Bn opposed the Normandy landings. Some of these units retreated into western Germany and joined XV SS Cossack Cavalry Corps. The 137th Bn deployed to northern Italy, but was soon disbanded.

The 622nd–625th Bns wore bright red 'Old French' left-sleeve shields (of 'heater' shape with a pointed base) with1–4 silver diagonal (from top left) stripes, even after transfer to German Fortress Gren Regiments. The Regt HQ and German cadre personnel of Fortress Gren Regt 360 wore a plain red shield with silver inner edging, below a large tin tank silhouette with a brass 'F'; this may have commemorated Panzer Bn (F) 102, which had operated flame-thrower tanks in Ukraine in June 1941. This badge was later replaced by the M1943 ROA arm shield, also worn by other Cossack units in France.

Three Cossack regts and 12 bns continued fighting on the Eastern Front. The 1st and 2nd Volunteer Don Regts fought in Ukraine and Belarus, later forming 1st Don *Plastun* Regt in the Cossack Settlement at Tolmezzo, Italy. The 557th and 573rd Bns (and possibly 12th Cossack Regt) helped form the German 37th Police Rifle Regt on 23 Nov 1943, fighting in Ukraine until disbandment on 6 Apr 1944. The 161st and 207th Bns were disbanded in 1943; 57th and 572nd Bns helped suppress the Warsaw Uprising in Aug 1944; and I/454th and 631st Bns fought in Ukraine before joining the 1st Cossack Div in Croatia. The 213rd, 443rd, 574th and 580th Bns had retreated into Germany by 1945.

1st Cossack Division

In March 1943 Cossacks were assembled at Kherson, southern Ukraine, for transfer to Mielau (now Mława, Poland), where the 1st Cossack Div *(1.Kozaken-Division)* was formally established on 21 Apr 1943. The recruits comprised volunteers, Red Army POWs and deserters, but also men from émigré communities which since 1917 had settled across Europe including in Czechoslovakia, France, Germany, Poland and Yugoslavia. All HQ officers, regt and bn commanders and specialist NCOs were

Table 3: Cossack formations & major units, 24 Aug 1941–8 May 1945

Cossack Cavalry Corps, Croatia:

- *XIV SS Cossack Cav Corps* (r. 9.1944): 1st & 2nd Cossack Cav Divs; 1.2.1945, became *XV SS Cossack Cav Corps*: 1st & 2nd Cossack Cav Divs, 3rd Cossack Div
- *1st Cossack Div* (r. 21.4.1943): 5.8.1943, I Cossack Mtd Bde (11.1.1944, became I Don Cossack Mtd Bde) – Cossack Mtd Regt 1, 2 & 3; 9.1943, Cossack Mtd Regts 1, 2 & 4, I Cossack Arty Bn 55; 5.8.1943, II Cossack Mtd Bde (11.1.1944, II Cossack Mtd Bde Caucasus) – Cossack Mtd Regts 4, 5 & 6; 9.1943, Cossack Mtd Regts 3, 5 & 6, II Cossack Arty Bn 55; div. services 55; (9.1944) became *1 Cossack Cav Div* – Cossack Mtd Regts 1, 2 & 4, Cossack Arty Regt 1
- *2nd Cossack Cav Div* (r. 9.1944) – Cossack Mtd Regts 3, 5 & 6; 25.2.1945, Cossack Mtd Regt 2
- *3rd Cossack Div* (r. 25.2.1945): III *Plastun* Bde – 7 & 8 *Plastun* Regts

Cossack Regiments:

- Cossack Hundred 102, GOC Rear Area, Army Group Centre (r. 22.8.1941, C. Russia); 7.1942, Cossack Bn 102; 28.9.1942, Cossack Bn 600; 12.7.1943, Cossack Mtd Regt 5, Generalgouvernement; 3.8.1943, Don Cossack Mtd Regt 5, Croatia; 25.2.1945, 7 *Plastun* Regt, W. Germany
- Fürst von Urach Mtd Bn (r. early 1942, S. Russia); 26.8.1942, Fürst von Urach Cav Regt; 15.8.1942, Von Jungschultz Cav Regt; 15.2.1943, Cossack Regt 1, S. Russia; 1.6.1943, 3 Sswodno Mtd Regt, Ukraine; 26.6.1943, 3 Sswodnyi Mtd Regt; 5.8.1943, Kuban Cossack Mtd Regt 3, Croatia
- Mtd Bn 454 (r. 1.8.1942, S. Russia); 29.10.1942, I & II/Eastern Mtd Bn 454; 1.4.1943, Eastern Mtd Regt 454 (I–IV Bns), Ukraine; 12.1944, disbanded
- Pannwitz Mtd Unit (r. 15.11.1942, S. Russia); 4.8.1943, HQ 1st Cossack Div, Generalgouvernement; 12.1944, HQ 1st Cossack Cav Div, Croatia
- Platov Cossack Regt (r. 6.1942, S. Russia); 17.6.1943, Light Cossack *(Plastun)* Bn 2; 1.8.1943, 2 Cossack Mtd Regt, Croatia; 5.8.1943, Ural Cossack Mtd Regt 2; 25.8.1943, Siberian Cossack Mtd Regt 2, Croatia
- Special Cossack Detachment (r. 6.1942, Ukraine); 9.1942, Belarus; 12.1942, 14 Mixed Cossack Regt; 11.9.1943, Cossack Bn 575, Ukraine; 4.1944, Cossack Bn/3 Cav Bde, Belarus; 12.1944, Cossack Bn 69, Generalgouvernement; 1945, to XV SS Cossack Cav Corps, Croatia
- 1 Ataman Regt (r. 6.6.1942, Ukraine); 4.8.1943, to I Cossack Mtd Bde, Croatia
- 2 Lifeguard Cossack Regt (r. 6.1942, Ukraine); 11.9.1943, Cossack Bn 570, Ukraine; 6.1944, N. France; 14.10.1944, disbanded
- 3 Don Cossack Regt (r. 7.1942, Ukraine); 1.1943, Don Cossack Bn 557; 5.8.1943, in 1st Cossack Cav Div, Croatia
- 4 Kuban Cossack Regt (r. 8.1942, Ukraine); 11.9.1943, Cossack Bn 571; 23.11.1943, to Police Rifle Regt 37, Ukraine; 6.4.1944, disbanded
- 5 Kuban Cossack Regt (r. 8.1942, Ukraine); spring 1943, 5 Kuban Cossack Cav Regt; 1.1944, to (Mtd)/Vol Cossack Depot Regt 5, N. France; 2.1945, to XV SS Cossack Cav Corps, Croatia
- 6 Mixed Cossack Regt (r. 8.1942, Ukraine); 3.12.1942, in OC Eastern Troops 703 (I & II Bns became Cossack Bns 622 & 623), C. Russia; 10.1943, in Regt HQ 750, W. France; 19.4.1944, I & II (Cossack) Bns/FGR 360; 9.1944, in Vol Cossack Depot Regt 5, N. France; 25.2.1945, in III *Plastun* Bde, E. Germany
- 7 Mixed Cossack Regt (r. 8.1942, Ukraine); 3.12.1942, in OC Eastern Troops 703 (I & II Bns became Cossack Bns 624 & 625); 10.1943, in Regt HQ 750, W. France; 19.4.1944, III (Cossack) Bns/FGRs 854 & 855; 14.10.1944, disbanded
- 8 Mixed Cossack Regt (r. 8.1942, Ukraine); 12.1942, Cossack Bn 631, C. Russia; 1.1945, to XV SS Cossack Cav Corps, Croatia
- 9 Kuban Cossack Regt (r. 9.1942, Ukraine); 1.1943, Kuban Cossack Bn 558; 8.1943, to Kuban Cossack Mtd Regt 4, Croatia
- 1 Volga Cossack Regt (r. 11.1942, S. Russia); 21.4.1943, Mława, Generalgouvernement; 13.5.1943, I Bn/6 Terek Cossack Mtd Regt, E. Germany
- 10 Don Cossack Regt (r. 12.1942, Ukraine); 1.1943, Belarus; 11.9.1943, Cossack Bn 573; 23.11.1943, to Police Rifle Regt 37, Ukraine; 6.4.1944, disbanded
- 11 Kuban Cossack Regt (r. 12.1942, Ukraine); 1.1943, Belarus; 11.9.1943, Cossack Bn 574; 1945, E. Germany
- 12 Mixed Cossack Regt (r. 12.1942, Belarus); 23.11.1943, to Police Rifle Regt 37, Ukraine; 6.4.1944, disbanded
- 1 & 2 Volunteer Don Cossack Regts (r. 1.1943, S. Russia); 2.1943, Ukraine; 1944, Belarus; 1945, 1 Don Cossack *Plastun* Regt, N. Italy
- 1 Sinegorsk Cossack Ataman Regt (r. 1.1943, S. Russia); 1.1943, Ukraine; 25.2.1943, to 1 Cossack Regt
- 1 Kuban Cav Regt (r. 1.1943, Ukraine); 21.4.1943, Mława, Generalgouvernement; 13.5.1943, to 4 Kuban Mtd Regt
- Kuban *Plastun* Bn (r. 1.1943, Ukraine); 3.1943, *Plastun* Regt; 21.4.1943, Mława, Generalgouvernement; 13.5.1943, to 1st Cossack Div
- 13 Mixed Cossack Regt; not formed; personnel formed 6 Cossack Regt (spring 1943)?
- 6 Cossack Regt (r. spring 1943, Ukraine); 9.11.1943, Cossack Bn 572, Belarus; 8.1944, Warsaw Uprising; 1945, to XV SS Cossack Cav Corps, Croatia
- 1 Don Mtd Regt (r. 11.5.1943, E. Germany); 5.8.1943, 1 Don Cossack Mtd Regt, Croatia
- 4 Kuban Mtd Regt (r. 13.5.1943, E. Germany); 5.8.1943, 4 Kuban Cossack Mtd Regt, Croatia
- 6 Terek Cossack Mtd Regt (r. 13.5.1943, E. Germany); 4.8.1943, Croatia
- Cossack Instruction & Training Regt 1 (r. 8.1943, Generalgouvernement); 1.2.1944, N. France; 17.3.1944, (Mtd)/Vol Cossack Depot Regt 5 (II Bn/Eastern Mtd Regt & Eastern Mtd Bn 403); 31.1.1945, Cossack Training & Replacement Regt, W. Germany
- (Cossack) Fortress Gren Regt 360 (r. 19.4.1944, W. France); 25.2.1945, III *Plastun* Bde, Croatia

German, but as a distinction all officers in Podpolkovnik Kononov's 5th Don Regt were Russian.

By Aug 1943 the 12,000-strong 1st Cossack Div, under GenMaj Helmuth von Pannwitz, comprised an HQ, including Pannwitz's Bodyguard Mtd Sqn; divisional HQ troops; a German-manned motorized recce bn with armoured cars, motorcycles, cars and trucks; and 2 mtd bdes with 6 mtd regts: 1st and 5th Don, 3rd and 4th Kuban, 6th Terek and 2nd Siberian, the last grouping Cossacks from the seven Asian hosts so far unrepresented. The 1st Cossack Div was always accompanied by soldiers' families in the baggage-train. The

Table 4: Cossack Battalions & Independent Cossack Corps, 24 Aug 1941–8 May 1945

Independent Cossack Battalions:

- 1 Mtd Hundred 213 (r. 20.10.1941, Ukraine); 6.4.1942, Mtd Bn 213; 15.10.1942, III (Cossack) Bn/Security Regt 57; 25.4.1943, Mtd Bn 57, Belarus; 8.1944, Warsaw Uprising; 1945, E. Germany
- Cossack Hundred 444 (r. winter 1941, S. Russia); 5.1942, 1 Mtd Bn 444, Ukraine; 29.10.1942, I (Eastern) Bn/Mtd Bn 444; 1.4.1943, III(Eastern) Bn/Mtd Regt 454, Ukraine; 4.1944, Mtd Bn 70, Generalgouvernement; 12.1944, in (Mtd)/Vol Cossack Depot Regt 5, N. France; 2.1945, to XV SS Cossack Cav Corps, Croatia
- 1–3 Cossack Sqns/MP Bn 581 (r. 1.11.1941, C. Russia); 2.4.1943, Eastern Mtd Bn 580; 4.1945, Russian Mtd Bn 580, E. Germany
- Mtd Bn 318 (r. spring 1942, Ukraine); 30.11.1942, Cossack Mtd Bn 213, Generalgouvernement; 1.1945, E. Germany
- Mtd Hundred 285 (r. 29.3.1942, N. Russia); 27.5.1942, Mtd Bn (Russian) 285; 23.10.1942, Eastern Mtd Bn 285; 10.10.1943, N. France; 4.12.1943, Eastern Bicycle Bn 285; 10.5.1945, surrendered, W. France (Ukrainian unit)
- Mtd Bn 207 (r. 11.4.1942, N. Russia); 31.10.1942, Eastern Mtd Bn 207; 1943, disbanded (Russian unit)
- Cossack Sqn 443 (r. 5. 5.1942, C. Russia); 15.1.1943, Cossack Mtd Bn 443; 12.1943, Belarus; 7.1944, Generalgouvernement; 1.1945, E. Germany
- 2 Mtd Bn 444 (r. 5.1942, Ukraine); 29.10.1942, II Bn/(Eastern) Mtd Bn 444; 1.4.1943, IV Bn (Eastern)/Mtd Regt 454, Ukraine; 1.1944, in (Mtd)/Vol Cossack Depot Regt 5 , N. France: 1945, W. Germany
- 1 Mtd Bn, 454 Security Div (r. 20.7.1942, S. Russia); 14.9.1942, Mtd Bn, 454 Security Div; 31.5.1943, Eastern Mtd Bn 403; 28.6.1944, III (Mtd) Bn/Cossack Depot Regt 5, N. France; 1945, to XV SS Cossack Cav Corps, Croatia
- Mtd Hundred 281 (r. summer 1942, N. Russia); 23.10.1942, Eastern Mtd Bn 281; 10.1943, N. France; 10.5.1945, surrendered, W. France (Ukrainian unit)
- Cossack Schutzmannschaft Bn (r. 7.1942, Ukraine); 1.1943, Cossack Bn 126; 5.1943, disbanded
- Mtd Bn 454 (r. 1.8.1942, S. Russia); 10.9.1942, 1 Mtd Bn 454; 29.10.1942, I Bn/(Eastern) Mtd Bn 454, S. Russia; 1.4.1943, I/(Eastern) Bn/Mtd Regt 454, Ukraine; early 1945, in 1 Cossack Cav Div, Croatia
- 2 Mtd Bn 454 (r. 10.9.1942, S. Russia); 29.10.1942, 2 Mtd Bn 454, S. Russia; 6.1944, II (Mtd) Bn/Vol Cossack Depot Regt 5, N. France; 9.1944, destroyed, N. France
- Cossack Mtd Bn 299 (r. 1942, S. Russia); probably 1 & 2 Sqns only
- Millerovo Sqn/Savoia Cav Regt (r. 1942, S. Russia); 25.9.1942, 'Savoia' Independent Cossack Bn; 3.1943, Italy; 9.9.1943, to German Army, N. Italy; 9.1944, to Cossack Settlement, N. Italy
- Cossack Bn 137 (r. 10.1942, C. Russia); autumn 1943, disbanded, N. Italy
- Cossack Bn 161 (r. 1943, Ukraine)
- Cossack Bn 575 (r. 2.1944); formation doubtful

Independent Cossack Corps – NE Italy:

- *Independent Cossack Corps* (r. 4.1945): HQ (*Plastun* Bn, MP Bn, Ataman Special Recce Group); 1 & 2 Cossack *Plastun* Div; 5.1945, disbanded
- *1 Cossack Plastun Div:* I Don Cossack *Plastun* Bde – 1 & 2 Don Cossack *Plastun* Regts; II Mixed Cossack *Plastun* Bde – 3 Kuban, 4 Terek-Stavropol Cossack *Plastun* Regts
- *2 Cossack Plastun Div*: III Mixed Cossack *Plastun* Bde – 5 Mixed, 6 Don Cossack *Plastun* Regts; IV Mixed Cossack *Plastun* Bde – 3 Cossack Reserve *Plastun* Regt; Independent Cossack Bn, 1 Cossack Cav Regt

1,000-strong Cossack Instruction & Training Regt *(Kozaken-Lehr und Ausbildungsregiment)* at Mokowo, later 5th Cossack Regt Volunteer Depot Div in France, included the various 'Young Cossack' cadet units.

A Mtd Regt *(Reiter-Regiment)* had 2,000 men and a 150-strong German cadre. It comprised an HQ, Sigs platoon, and 9th Heavy Sqn with 2 AT platoons (3 guns each) and 2 mortar platoons (4 medium mortars each); and 2 bns (I–II), 2 of which (II/2 and II/5) were bicycle battalions. A Mtd Bn had an HQ and Sigs section; 3 Mtd Sqns (1–3 or 5–7), each with 3 platoons (3 light MGs each) and a troop (2 heavy MGs); and a Heavy Sqn with 2 MG platoons (4 MGs each) and a mortar platoon (4 medium mortars). A Bde Horse Arty Bn had an HQ, HQ bty, and 3 btys each with 4 field guns.

The 1st Cossack Div was the largest ex-Soviet formation yet permitted by the Germans, but Hitler refused Pannwitz's request to fight on the Eastern Front, diverting him instead to 2nd Pz Army in Croatia to fight Tito's Partisans. Thus in mid-Sept 1943 the division left Mława by train and in early Oct established its HQ at Syrmia at Hrvatska Mitrovica (now Sremska Mitrovica, Serbia). The Cossacks engaged Partisan units in the Fruška Gora region inconclusively, and the first cases emerged of desertion, poor discipline, and mistreatment of the local Croatian (in theory, allied) civilian population. From mid-October the division guarded the strategic Zagreb–Belgrade railway line west of Vinkovci. In late November, I Bde diverted to Petrinja, near Zagreb, where it retook the Glina area, but only after the 2nd Siberian Regt had suffered a mauling. Meanwhile, II Bde fought near Doboj, northern Bosnia.

In Jan 1944 the division reassembled near Karlovac, south of Zagreb. On 29 March, 2nd Siberian Regt and the Recce Bn destroyed a Partisan brigade near Sisak, and in April the 2nd Siberian Regt fought at Karlovac. On 1 Apr, Pannwitz was promoted Generalleutnant. In May 1944 the Div HQ moved to Nova Gradiška, and I Bde deployed around Sisak and Glina south of Zagreb. On 29 June, II Bde's 3rd Kuban and 5th Don Regts operated at Đakovo and Ruševo in Slavonia, on 26 July at Prnjavor in northern Bosnia, and in mid-August at Daruvar, western Slavonia. Meanwhile, I Bde captured Metlika on the Slovene-Croatian border on 15 July.

XIV Cossack Cavalry Corps

On 26 Aug 1944, Himmler, as commander of the Replacement Army, promised increased equipment and supplies and expansion to a corps if Pannwitz agreed to transfer 1st Cossack Div to the Waffen-SS. Thus, in late Sept 1944 the formation was redesignated *XIV. SS-Kosaken-Kavallerie-Korps*, with I and II Bdes renamed 1st & 2nd Cossack Cav Divs, retaining the existing battle-order but adding reinforcements from independent Cossack units. Pannwitz was nominally promoted SS-Gruppenführer, but the Corps remained under German Army control and did not adopt Waffen-SS uniforms or insignia.

In early Oct 1944, 2nd Div captured Banja Luka, western Bosnia, while 1st Div moved to Kutina, northern Croatia on 20 October. On 10 Dec, 2nd Div reached Koprivnica and, advancing along the Drava Valley in northern Slavonia, took Klostar on the 23rd and defeated the Red Army 133rd Rifle Div at Pitomača on 26 Dec, but failed to capture Virovitica on 5 Jan 1945. On 7 Jan, 1st Div advanced east from Kutina, blocking Partisan forces at Lipik and Pakrac.

XV Cossack Cavalry Corps

On 1 Feb 1945 the 25,000-strong XIV Corps was renumbered XV Corps; and 3rd Cossack Div was established on 25 Feb with infantrymen from Obstlt von Renteln's 360th Fortress Gren Regt from France, redesignated III *Plastun* Bde under Polkovnik Kononov. By early March, Corps HQ was established at Podravka Slatina in the southern Drava Valley, with 1st and 2nd Divs at Virovitica and Suhopolje respectively. The 4th Kuban Regt established a bridgehead over the Drava at Valpovo.

During March and April 1945, XV Corps remained on the Drava resisting Partisan and Red Army attacks. On 1 Apr, Kononov was promoted Generalmayor, and on 28 Apr Gen Vlasov accepted XV Corps into the VS-KONR, appointing Kononov commander of all anti-Soviet Cossacks on 5 May. Meanwhile, on 13 Apr, Gen Pannwitz was elected 'Field Chieftain *(Pokhodny ataman)* of all Cossack Hosts', the supreme Cossack office historically reserved for the Tsar.

At the end of Apr 1945 the 18,000-strong XV Corps retreated from the southern Drava Valley, briefly holding up the enemy advance at Koprivnica on 4–6 May, before falling back into southern Austria at Lavamünd pursued by the Bulgarian 1st Army. Corps HQ, 2nd and 3rd Divs encamped at Althofen, 1st Div at Feldkirchen. On 8 May, Gen Pannwitz, undefeated in battle, surrendered to British 8th Army. From 29 May XV Corps was handed over to the Red Army for repatriation and punishment. Pannwitz voluntarily followed his comrades, and was hanged in Moscow on 16 Jan 1947.

A member of the 1st Cossack Div's Bodyguard Mtd Sqn, commanded by *Khorunzhiy* Boitshevsky, talks to a German NCO after a parade in Sisak, Croatia, February 1944. The ceremonial uniform was a black *kubanka* cap, red *beshmet* shirt, black *cherkeska* coat, red *bashlyk* hood (note supporting cords round the neck), with a silver-mounted *kindzhal* dagger. The cap bears the metal insignia from a German M1935 peaked service cap; the red *beshmet* has black piping and small black buttons, and the *cherkeska* has pointed red shoulder straps and sets of ten cartridge-tubes on the breast. For the squadron's field uniform, see Plate G1. (Tchakov Collection)

Cossack Division distinctive uniforms and insignia

The 1st Cossack Div wore German field-grey uniforms as previously described, and was able to achieve a greater uniformity than in the independent units. Personnel from the newly formed Siberian Cossack Regt wore a yellow (inner) and blue cap cockade; M1943 officers' service-dress shoulder straps were silver with blue piping and yellow centre-stripes, and NCOs' and men's straps were yellow piped in blue. The tall *papacha* cap was of white fleece with a yellow cloth top, although Don and Siberian Cossacks could also wear low *kubanka* caps.

The *papacha* and *kubanka* caps had host-colour crowns, initially decorated with a plain silver-braid cross (not for Don Cossacks) or more elaborate designs, some cap crowns having braid and cord edging denoting rank. Cap badges usually comprised the metal eagle-and-swastika above a German cockade in an oak-leaf wreath, as worn on the German M1935 service cap, but these might be replaced with an M1943 Cossack host oval cockade. Lambswool caps were worn squarely on the brow, but off duty could be pushed off the forehead, exposing the traditional *chub* (Don) or *cholka* (Kuban) curling quiff of hair at the temples.

General Pannwitz's divisional Bodyguard Mtd Sqn (the traditional Russian *Konvoi*) was commanded by Khorunzhiy (later Yesaul) Boitshevsky; plans to form a 4-sqn bn were never realized. The Bodyguard wore a Caucasian parade uniform, comprising a black *kubanka* with a red cloth crown but no badges; red *beshmet* shirt piped black; black *cherkeska* coat with red lining (subalterns: narrow silver-braid cuff, collar, and shirt-front edging); M1943 Kuban service-dress shoulder straps, and two gold-braid cuff chevrons points-up (sometimes omitted); and a red *bashlyk* hood piped black. The field tunic had red Kuban shoulder straps with gold-braid NCO rank bars, the cuff chevrons (also worn on the greatcoat), and a blue oval cloth badge on the right upper sleeve depicting a gold Ataman's mace between two *shashqa* swords. On ceremonial occasions other Kuban and Terek Cossacks wore a Caucasian uniform in various colours. Oberst Konstantin Wagner, commanding 1st Don Regt, also had a bodyguard unit, whose personnel wore a large green cloth chevron point-down on the left upper sleeve of the field tunic and greatcoat.

The range of arm shields were standardized and expanded. Shields were now usually worn on the right upper sleeve of the field tunic, but from Aug 1943 Don and Kuban Cossacks and horse artillery used either sleeve to distinguish different units. Dark bluish-green 'Spanish' arm shields with white superscriptions and coloured diagonal quarterings were introduced on 21 Apr 1943 for troops training at Mława:

Don, 4th pattern: 'DON' above red and blue
Kuban, 4th pattern: 'KUBAN' above red and black
Terek, 3rd pattern: 'TEREK' above mid-blue and black.

The white superscriptions were modified on 29 May 1943:

Don, 5th pattern: 'в д' (for *Voysko Donskoye* – Don Host)

Kuban, 5th pattern: 'K B' (*Kubanskoye Voysko* – Kuban Host)

Terek, 4th pattern: 'T B' (*Tverskoye Voysko* – Terek Host)

Siberian: 'п C B' (*Polk Sibirski Voyna Voysko* – Siberian Host Wartime Regt), above yellow and blue quarterings.

The 5th Recce Bn had a yellow and black quartered shield. Divisional HQ troops wore a 'Polish' shield with yellow-red-blue stripes on a black background; the Eng, Sigs and Horse Arty bns added to this black, yellow and red vertical cloth bars. II/55 Arty Bn had a red diagonal bar (top right), but scarcity of this shield meant that almost identical Don 1st-pattern shields were often substituted.

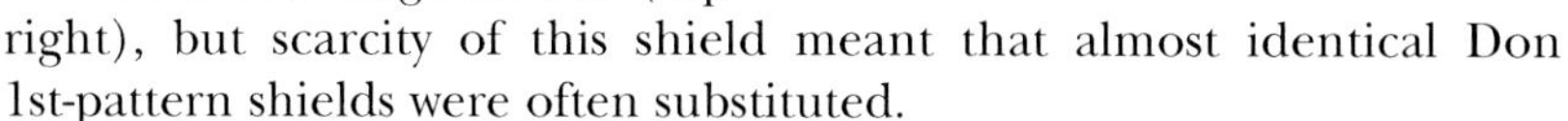

A soldier from 1st Cossack Cav Div poses for a propaganda photograph in a Croatian forest, March 1945; just visible on his right upper sleeve is the yellow-blue-red horizontally striped shield of the divisional troops. Although he wears an M1935 black belt with rifle-clip pouches, he poses with a Soviet PPSh-41 sub-machine gun, and has a belt of MG42 link ostentatiously draped over his shoulders. (Bundesarchiv, Bild 101I-198-1394-10A/CC-BY-SA)

From summer 1944, 5th Don Regt personnel wore a red, white and black regimental cross on the right breast pocket; and in May 1944, 2nd Siberian Regt adopted a blue and yellow enamel commemorative cross. Cossacks could qualify for a 'proficiency badge' comprising a gold-braid bar worn immediately above the arm shield.

Coloured piping or stripes were worn on German field-grey trousers and breeches and Cossack royal-blue breeches: Div HQ Troops, red piping; Recce Bn, plain trousers; Don, 5cm red stripe; Kuban, 2.5cm red stripe; Terek, narrow blue stripe edged black; Siberian, 5cm yellow stripe; Artillery, two narrow red stripes.

The Cossack Settlement, 1943–45

The Cossack Settlement at Navahrudak comprised Cossack families led by Sergey Pavlov, elected Field Ataman, commanding 4 Cossack regts – 1st and 2nd Don *Plastun*, 3rd Kuban Mtd and 4th Terek *Plastun* – which, though essentially only a militia, effectively protected the Settlement from Partisan attacks. The much-loved Pavlov was killed on 17 June 1944 under mysterious circumstances, and was succeeded by Polkovnik (later General-mayor) Timotei I. Domanov. In Sept 1944, as the Red Army advanced through Belarus, the 24,000-strong Settlement trekked 960 miles south to a new home at Tolmezzo in the north-east corner of the Italian Social Republic (*Repubblica Sociale Italiana* – RSI), just over the border from south-east Austria.

Two rather elderly-looking members of the Cossack Settlement militia stand guard in a small town between Tolmezzo and Gemona, north-east Italy, 1944. In stark contrast to ROA and Cossack Cavalry Corps personnel, they wear no insignia on their German M1941 tunics – no collar patches or shoulder straps, nor any sleeve badges. While they retain Cossack riding boots and carry slung Kar 98k rifles, they have no belts or other equipment. (Tchakov Collection)

Domanov's Cossacks fought alongside German and RSI forces across Friuli and Venezia Giulia provinces against Italian partisans. The 'Savoia' Independent Cossack Sqn, the only Cossack unit raised by any of Germany's allies, was formed by the Italian Expeditionary Corps in southern Russia in 1942; it retreated to Italy with its sponsors in March 1943, and joined Domanov in Sept 1944. In Apr 1945 the Field Ataman organized his 18,395 troops into a division-sized Independent Cossack Corps *(Otdel'niy Kazachiy Korpus)*, the principal units being the Corps HQ troops and 1st and 2nd Cossack *Plastun* Divs, each with 4 regts divided between 2 bdes, totalling 2 mtd regts (1st Cossack, 3rd Kuban), 5 *Plastun* regts (1st, 2nd & 6th Don, 3rd Reserve, 4th Terek), and 1 mixed regt (5th).

Threatened by the advancing British 8th Army and increasingly confident Italian partisans, Domanov, accompanied by Gens Pyotr and Simon Krasnov and later Andrei Shkuro, withdrew the Cossack civilians 50 miles north into Austria on 28 Apr 1945, led by mounted Cossacks with *Plastun* regts forming the rearguard, and set up camps around Lienz on 3 May. After fruitless negotiations the British forcibly sent the Cossack troops eastwards by train to the Soviet Zone of Austria on 1–15 June, to meet their grisly fate, while allowing the civilians to go free. Domanov, Shkuro and the Krasnovs were hanged in Moscow on 16 Jan 1947.

Domanov's personnel, led by German Police and Cossack Administration officers, were often older or younger and worse-equipped than Pannwitz's forces, and more individualistic in their uniforms. Headgear comprised *papacha* and *kubanka* caps, pre-1917 blue peaked caps with host-colour bands, German M1935 officers' service caps, M1938 officers' and M1934 and M1942 enlisted ranks' sidecaps, and M1943 peaked field caps, with German Army and Police (for the MP Bn) cap badges and Tsarist black-and-orange cockades. German M1940, M1941 and M1943 field-grey tunics were worn with pre-1917 Tsarist shoulder straps, plain collars or German M1935 officers' and M1938 or M1940 enlisted ranks' collar patches. Unit badges included the M1938 Waffen-SS silver-grey woven eagle-and-swastika or the MP Bn's M1943 Police-green Schutzpolizei badge on the left upper sleeve; a black M1943 Waffen-SS 'New French' shield (of squat shape, with a shallow-pointed 'scalloped' base), with a white 'ACB' (*Astrakhanskoe Sibirski Voysko* – Astrakhan Siberian Host) superscription above red and white quarterings for Astrakhan Cossacks; and a Russian white-red-blue horizontally striped 'New French' shield on the right upper sleeve. However, a lack of badges and decorations contrasted with other Cossack units. Caucasian uniform was worn for parades. The 'Savoia' Sqn wore a white *kubanka* cap with red crown and red (inner) and white oval cockade; Italian M1940 greyish-green uniform with white Novara Lancers three-flame regimental collar patches; and a white (top)-blue-red cloth chevron on the right upper arm.

SELECT BIBLIOGRAPHY

De Lannoy, François, *Les Cosaques de Pannwitz/Pannwitz Cossacks 1942–1945* (Heimdal; Château de Damigny, 2000)

Littlejohn, David, *Foreign Legions of the Third Reich, Vol 4* (Bender Publishing; San Jose, CA, 1987)

Schlicht, Adolf & Angolia, John R., *Die Deutsche Wehrmacht; Band 1, das Heer* (Motorbuch Verlag; Stuttgart, 1996)

Schuster, Peter & Tiede, Harald, *Uniforms and Insignia of the Cossacks in the German Wehrmacht* (Schiffer; Atglen, PA, 2003)

Thorwald, Jürgen, *The Illusion: Soviet Soldiers in Hitler's Armies* (Houghton Mifflin Harcourt; Boston, MA, 1978)

Table 5: Russian rank insignia,1 Aug 1942–8 May 1945

RNNA 1.9.1942–5.1943 (khaki shoulder straps, gold stripes, red badges)	Security Units (1) 20.8.1942–28.5.1943 (red collar patches/red, later field-grey shoulder straps)	ROA Infantry (1) 29.5.1943–11.5.1945 (dark bluish-green shoulder straps)	ROA Infantry (1) 18.3.1944–8.5.1945 (German Army shoulder straps)	British Army equivalent
***General officers*:**				
-	-	**General (2)** *(gold zigzag, 2 silver stars)*	**General (2)** *(gold/silver/gold plait, 2 silver stars)*	Lieutenant- General
-	-	**General-leytenant** *(gold zigzag, 1 silver star)*	**General-leytenant** *(gold/silver/gold plait, 1 silver star)*	Major-General
-	-	**General-mayor** *(gold zigzag)*	**General-mayor** *(gold/silver/gold plait)*	Brigadier
***Field officers*:**				
Polkovnik *(2 stripes, 4 bars)*	-	**Polkovnik** *(2 stripes, 2 gold stars)*	**Polkovnik** *(silver plait, 2 gold stars)*	Colonel
Podpolkovnik *(2 stripes, 3 bars)*	-	**Podpolkovnik** *(2 stripes, 1 gold star)*	**Podpolkovnik** *(silver plait, 1 gold star)*	Lieutenant- Colonel
Mayor *(2 stripes, 2 bars)*	**Bataillonsführer (2)** *(silver edging, 1 bar, 2 stars/ silver strap, 2 knots)*	**Mayor** *(2 stripes)*	**Mayor** *(silver plait)*	Major
***Subaltern officers*:**				
Kapitan *(2 stripes, 1 bar)*	**Kompanieführer** *(silver edging, 1 bar, 1 star/ silver strap, 1 knot)*	**Kapitan** *(1 stripe, 2 gold stars)*	**Kapitan** *(flat silver braid, 2 gold stars)*	Captain
Starshiy leytenant *(1 stripe, 3 squares)*	**Stellvertretender Kompanieführer** *(silver edging, 1 bar/silver strap)*	**Poruchik** *(1 stripe, 1 gold star)*	**Poruchik** *(flat silver braid, 1 gold star)*	Lieutenant
Leytenant *(1 stripe, 2 squares)*	-	**Podporuchik** *(1 stripe)*	**Podporuchik** *(flat silver braid)*	2nd Lieutenant
Mladshiy leytenant *(1 stripe, 1 square)*	-	-	-	-
***Non-commissioned officers*:**				
-	**Zugführer** *(silver edging/2 stripes)*	-	-	WO1
	Hauptfeldwebel (3) *(2 cuff rings)*	**Hauptfeldwebel (3)** *(2 cuff rings)*	**Khaupt-fel'dfebel' (3)** *(2 cuff rings)*	WO2 (CSM)
Starshina *(3 triangles)*	-	-	**Ober-fel'dfebel' (5)** *(silver-braid edging, 2 silver stars)*	Colour Sergeant
Starshiy serzhant *(2 triangles)*	**Stellvertretender Zugführer** *(silver chevron, 2 bars / 3 bars)*	**Feldwebel** *(3 bars)*	**Fel'dfebel'** *(silver-braid edging, 1 silver star)*	Sergeant
Mladshiy serzhant *(1 triangle)*	**Gruppenführer** *(silver chevron, 1 bar/2 bars)*	**Unteroffizier** *(2 bars)*	**Unter-ofitser** *(silver-braid outer edging)*	Corporal
***Men*:**				
-	-	**Obergefreiter (4)** *(1bar, 1 silver star)*	**Ober-yefreytor** *(2 silver arm chevrons)*	-
	Stellvertretender Gruppenführer *(silver chevron/1 bar)*	**Gefreiter** *(1 bar)*	**Yefreytor** *(1 silver arm chevron)*	Lance- Corporal
-	-	**Oberschütze (4)** *(1 silver star)*	**Ober-soldat** *(1 silver arm star)*	-
Ryadovoy *(plain strap)*	**Schütze** *(plain patch/plain strap)*	**Freiwilliger** *(plain strap)*	**Soldat** *(plain strap)*	Private

Notes: (1) For the 'Mtd' cavalry rank titles, see Table 6. (2) Rank created but never held. (3) An appointment held by an NCO acting as Company Sergeant-Major. (4) Introduced 1 Jan 1944. (5) Introduced 15 June 1944.

Table 6: Cossack rank insignia, 20 Aug 1942–8 May 1945

Cossacks, less Russian Army 9.11.1917 *Silver-braid/cloth shoulder straps)*	Security Units (1) 20.8.1942–28.5.1943 *(silver-braid/red, later field-grey shoulder straps) (2)*	Cossack Cavalry (1) 29.5.1943–8.5.1945 *(dark bluish-green shoulder straps)*	Cossack Cavalry (1) 18.3.1944–8.5.1945 *(German Army shoulder straps)*	British Army equivalent
***General officers*:**				
General ot kavalerii *(braid only)*	-	-	-	General
General-leytenant *(braid, 3 gold stars)*	-	**General (3)** *(gold zigzag, 2 silver stars)*	**General (3)** *(gold/silver/gold plait, 2 silver stars)*	Lieutenant-General
General-mayor *(braid, 2 gold stars)*	-	**General-leytenant (3)** *(gold zigzag, 1 silver star)*	**General-leytenant (3)** *(gold/silver/gold plait, 1 silver star)*	Major-General
-	-	**General-mayor (3)** *(gold zigzag)*	**General-mayor** *(gold/silver/gold plait)*	Brigadier
***Field officers*:**				
Polkovnik *(braid, 2 stripes)*		**Polkovnik** *(2 stripes, 2 gold stars)*	**Polkovnik** *(silver plait, 2 gold stars)*	Colonel
Voyskovoy starshina *(braid, 2 stripes, 3 stars)*		**Voyskovoy starshina** *(2 stripes, 1 gold star)*	**Voyskovoy starshina** *(silver plait, 1 gold star)*	Lieutenant- Colonel
-	**Abteilungsführer (2)** *(silver edging, 1 bar, 2 stars/silver strap, 2 knots)*	**Mayor** *(2 stripes)*	**Mayor** *(silver plait)*	Major
***Subaltern officers*:**				
Yesaul (1) *(braid, 1 stripe)*	-	-	-	Captain
Pod'esaul *(braid, 1 stripe, 4 stars)*	**Schwadronsführer** *(silver edging, 1 bar, 1 star/silver strap, 1 knot)*	**Yesaul** *(1 stripe, 2 gold stars)*	**Yesaul** *(flat silver braid, 2 gold stars)*	
Sotnik *(braid, 1 stripe, 3 stars)*	**Stellvertretender Schwadronsführer** *(silver edging,1 bar/silver strap)*	**Sotnik** *(1 stripe, 1 gold star)*	**Sotnik** *(flat silver braid, 1 gold star)*	Lieutenant
Khorunzhiy *(braid, 1 stripe, 2 stars)*	-	**Khorunzhiy** *(1 stripe)*	**Khorunzhiy** *(flat silver braid)*	2nd Lieutenant
***Non-commissioned officers*:**				
Zauryad khorunzhiy *(cloth, thick bar & thick stripe)*	-	-	-	-
Podkhorunzhiy *(cloth, thick stripe)*	**Zugführer** *(silver edging/2 stripes)*	-	-	WO1
Vakhmistr *(cloth, thick bar)*	**Hauptwachtmeister (4)** *(2 cuff rings)*	**Hauptwachtmeister (4)** *(2 cuff rings)*	**Khaupt-vakhmistr (4)** *(2 cuff rings)*	WO2 (SSM)
-	-	-	**Ober-vakmistr (6)** *(silver-braid edging, 2 silver stars)*	Staff Sergeant
Starshiy uryadnik *(cloth, 3 bars)*	**Stellvertretender Zugführer** *(silver chevron, 2 bars/3 bars)*	**Wachtmeister** *(3 bars)*	**Vakhmistr** *(silver-braid edging, 1 silver star)*	Sergeant
Mladshiy uryadnik *(cloth, 2 bars)*	**Gruppenführer** *(silver chevron, 1 bar/2 bars)*	**Unteroffizier** *(2 bars)*	**Uryadnik** *(silver outer braid)*	Corporal
***Men*:**				
-	-	**Obergefreiter (5)** *(1bar, 1 silver star)*	**Starshiy prikasni** *(2 silver arm chevrons)*	
Prikasni *(cloth, 1 bar)*	**Stellvertretender Gruppenführer** *(silver chevron/1 bar)*	**Gefreiter** *(1 bar)*	**Prikasni** *(1 silver arm chevron)*	Lance- Corporal
-	-	**Oberreiter (5)** *(1 silver star)*	**Starshiy kazak** *(1 silver arm star)*	-
Kazak *(plain cloth strap)*	**Reiter** *(plain patch/plain strap)*	**Reiter** *(plain strap)*	**Kazak** *(plain strap)*	Trooper

Notes: (1) Cavalry ranks are shown. For 'dismounted' rank titles of Cossack infantry, see Table 5. (2) The Security Bn collar patches were replaced by crossed-lances collar patches from 15 Nov 1942. (3) Rank created but never held. (4) An appointment held by an NCO acting as Squadron Sergeant-Major. (5) Rank introduced 1 Jan 1944. (6) Rank introduced 15 June 1944.

Table 7: Cossack arm shields, 15 Nov 1942–8 May 1945

Cossack Unit	Date introduced	Shield shape	Description	Upper sleeve
Von Jungschultz Regt	1943?	Old French	Black, silver-wire Prussian skull	Left
1 Cossack Div/(9.1944) Corps HQ (1)	Autumn 1943	Oval	Dark blue, red inner piping; gold Ataman's mace between gold and black swords	Right
Divisional/Corps HQ Troops (2)	Autumn 1943	Polish	Yellow-blue-red stripes	Right
Don Cossacks (1st pattern)	15 Nov 1942	Spanish	Yellow-blue-red stripes	Left
Don Cossacks (2nd ptn)	1942–43 (unofficial)	Spanish	Red (top/bottom) and blue (sides) diagonal quartering	Left
Don Cossacks (3rd ptn)	1942–43 (unofficial)	Polish	Blue 'DON' above yellow-blue-red stripes	Left
Don Cossacks (4th ptn)	21 Apr 1943	Spanish	White 'DON' above red and blue diagonal quartering, on dark bluish-green	Left
Don Cossacks (5th ptn)	29 May 1943	Spanish	White 'вд' above red and blue diagonal quartering, on dark bluish-green	Left
Don Cossack Regts 1 & 5 (5th ptn)	5 Aug 1943	Spanish	White 'вд' above red and blue diagonal quartering, on dark bluish-green	Right (1 Regt) Left (5 Regt)
Kuban Cossacks (1st ptn)	15 Nov 1942	Spanish	Yellow and green diagonal quartering	Left
Kuban Cossacks (2nd ptn)	1942 (unofficial)	Polish	Yellow 'KUBAN' above green and yellow diagonal quartering	Left
Kuban Cossacks (3rd ptn)	1942–43 (unofficial)	Spanish	Red and black diagonal quartering	Left
Kuban Cossacks (4th ptn)	21 Apr 1943	Spanish	White 'KUBAN' above red and black diagonal quartering, on dark bluish-green	Left
Kuban Cossacks (5th ptn)	29 May 1943	Spanish	White 'KB' above red and black diagonal quartering, on dark bluish-green	Left
Kuban Cossack Regts 3 & 4 (5th ptn)	5 Aug 1943	Spanish	White 'KB' above red and black diagonal quartering, on dark bluish-green	Left (3 Regt) Right (4 Regt)
Terek Cossacks (1st ptn)	15 Nov 1942	Spanish	Black-green-red stripes	Left
Terek Cossacks (2nd ptn)	1942–43 (unofficial)	Polish	Green 'TEREK' above black-green-red stripes	Left
Terek Cossacks (3rd ptn)	21 Apr 1943	Spanish	White 'TEREK' above mid-blue and black diagonal quartering, on dark bluish-green	Left
Terek Cossack Regt 6 (4th ptn)	5 Aug 1943	Spanish	White 'TB' above mid-blue and black diagonal quartering, on dark bluish-green	Left
Siberian Cossack Regt 2	25 Aug 1943	Spanish	Yellow 'псв' above yellow and blue diagonal quartering. on dark bluish-green	Right
Divisional Recce Bn 5	8 Apr 1944	Spanish	Yellow and black diagonal quartering, on dark bluish-green	Right
I/55 Horse Artillery Bn	Autumn 1943	Polish	Vertical red bar on yellow-blue-red stripes	Right
II/55 Horse Arty Bn	Autumn 1943	Polish	Diagonal red bar on yellow-blue-red stripes	Left
Cossack Eng Bn 55	Autumn 1943	Polish	Vertical black bar on yellow-blue-red stripes	Right
Cossack Sigs Bn 55	Autumn 1943	Polish	Vertical black bar on yellow-blue-red stripes	Right
Cossack Fortress Gren Regt 360	19 Apr 1944	Old French	Bright red, silver-wire inner edging	Left
Cossack Bn 622 (I/FGR 360)	3 Dec 1942	Old French	Bright red, silver-wire diagonal stripe	Left
Cossack Bn 623 (II/FGR 360)	3 Dec 1942	Old French	Bright red, 2 silver-wire diagonal stripes	Left
Cossack Bn 624 (III/FGR 854)	3 Dec 1942	Old French	Bright red, 3 silver-wire diagonal stripes	Left
Cossack Bn 625 (III/FGR 855)	3 Dec 1942	Old French	Bright red, 4 silver-wire diagonal stripes	Left
Astrakhan Cossacks	1943	New French	White 'ACB' above red and white diagonal quartering, on black	Left

Notes: All diagonal quarterings are given as colour of top & bottom quarters first, colour of side quarters second. (1) Bodyguard Sqn, Trumpet Band, MP Troop, Motorcycle Courier Platoon. (2) Medical Bn, Veterinary Co, Div Supply and Cossack Replacement Regt.

PLATE COMMENTARIES

A: RUSSIAN VOLUNTEER UNITS, 1941–42

A1: *Hilfswilliger*, German 36th Motorized Division; Kalinin, October 1941

This 'voluntary assistant' wears a Red Army M1927 khaki *budenovka* cap with badges removed, but retaining flap buttons in infantry crimson. As a two-month probationary soldier the shoulder straps have been removed from his German M1935 field-grey greatcoat, and he wears the white M1941 armband lettered *'Im Dienst/der/Deutsche Wehrmacht'*. His Russian M1912 belt has a single ammunition pouch for his 7.62mm M1891 Mosin-Nagant rifle.

A2: *Kapitan*, Russian Nationalist People's Army; Osintorf, July 1942

This company commander wears the M1935 *pilotka* field cap with the RNNA cockade and officers' gold piping. The M1929 officers' field shirt has red collar- and cuff-piping, and officers' service-dress collar patches; the M1942 RNNA shoulder straps are piped red, with two wide lengthways gold stripes and a yellow-edged red enamel rank bar. He has M1935 red-piped royal-blue officers' breeches, and the M1935 belt and cross-brace support a holstered 7.62mm M1895 Mosin-Nagant revolver.

A3: *Kompanieführer*, 601st Beresina Eastern Battalion; Bobruisk, November 1942

This company commander (an unusually high rank for a Russian) wears a German enlisted ranks' field cap with the Security units' M1942 badge of a red bar on a blue oval. His German M1941 enlisted ranks' tunic has the regulation Russian volunteers' collar patches, shoulder straps and 'winged swastika' breast badge, and he sports the ribbon and swords of the Eastern Decoration for Bravery 2nd Class in Silver. The rest of his clothing and equipment is German issue.

B: INDEPENDENT RUSSIAN VOLUNTEER UNITS, 1943–44

B1: *Feldwebel*, 1st Infantry Regiment, Special Division R; Pruskow, December 1944

This German cadre NCO wears the M1934 'old style' peaked field cap. His M1943 tunic has the silver *Tresse* braid and shoulder-strap star of his rank, and on his left sleeve a 'New French'-shaped divisional arm shield with gold piping and white-blue-red horizontal stripes. He displays the buttonhole-ribbon of the Iron Cross 2nd Class, and the pin-back Anti-Partisan War Badge in bronze. His M1943 trousers are gathered into M1940 'retreat' anklets above M1934 ankle boots, and his M1935 belt supports triple canvas magazine pouches for his MP40 sub-machine gun.

B2: *Podporuchik*, Armoured Battalion, Russian People's Liberation Army; Lokot, August 1943

This platoon commander from the T-34 battalion of the

April 1944: Bronisław V. Kaminski (right foreground) with RONA troops at Lepel, northern Belarus. Kaminski wears a German M1935 service cap with an M1943 ROA officers' cockade, and a six-button M1941 German enlisted ranks' field tunic with a plain dark bluish-green collar added, but no shoulder straps. He displays the M1943 RONA left-arm shield, and on his left pocket the Iron Cross 1st Class, Eastern Decoration 1st Class in Silver, and black Wound Badge. *Poruchik* Alexey Bagaturia (left foreground), a platoon leader in a RONA transport company, wears a Red Army M1935 peaked cap without insignia, and M1943 ROA officers' collar patches and shoulder straps. (Bundesarchiv, Bild 101I-280-1075-10A/Wehmeyer/CC-BY-SA)

infamous 'Kaminski Brigade' wears German armoured troops' black uniform with a mix of ROA and RONA insignia. His M1934 field-grey field cap bears the M1943 ROA officers' red-blue-silver oval cockade. The M1942 jacket has M1943 ROA officers' dark bluish-green collar patches with silver distinctions, and shoulder straps of the same colour with red piping and centre-stripe, but the M1943 RONA arm shield. Note too the buttonhole-ribbon of the Eastern Decoration 2nd Class in Bronze.

B3: *Unteroffizier*, 1st Guards Brigade, Russian Liberation Army; Pskov, June 1943

This NCO, formerly with the SS-Drushina Unit, wears a field-grey 'SD' uniform with ROA insignia. The field cap has an M1943 ROA officers' red-blue-silver cockade. His M1937 tunic has M1943 ROA enlisted ranks' collar patches, red-piped dark bluish-green shoulder straps with two silver rank bars, and the M1943 ROA arm shield. He has a grey shirt and black

SD tie, with M1937 trousers bloused over ankle boots, a German M1935 belt and pouches, and an M1891 Mosin-Nagant rifle.

C: RUSSIAN LIBERATION ARMY, 1943–44

C1: *General-leytenant* Georgiy N. Zhilenkov; Pskov, June 1943

General Vlasov's deputy wears regulation M1943 ROA general officers' field-grey uniform. The service cap has gold piping and cords, and the ROA officers' red-blue-silver badge on the dark bluish-green band. The German M1935 tunic has gold buttons; a dark bluish-green collar and tongue-shaped collar patches with gold button, piping and braid; dark bluish-green shoulder straps piped red, with a silver star on the gold zigzag braid; and an M1943 ROA arm shield. The breeches have red piping between red stripes. Zhilenkov has a German officers' field belt and hard-shell holster.

C2: Andrey A. Vlasov, Belarus, April 1943

Vlasov is wearing his rankless M1943 dark grey uniform with silver buttons and light grey trim. The peaked cap has the M1943 ROA officers' red-blue-silver cockade badge and silver cords. The six-button tunic had light grey piping at the collar, front and cuffs; three cuff buttons; and four external pleated pockets with buttoned, scalloped flaps. The greatcoat has light grey collar- and cuff-piping and lapel lining, and two rows of six buttons. The long trousers and his alternative breeches had two wide light grey stripes. In 1944 Vlasov adopted a dark brown uniform with gold buttons and cap piping, red piping to the tunic and greatcoat, red coat lapel lining, and red trouser- and breeches-stripes.

C3: *Fel'dfebel'*, 635th Eastern Battalion; Carentan, Normandy, June 1944

This deputy platoon commander resisting the Normandy landings wears a German M1943 tunic; the M1943 ROA dark bluish-green collar patches have a silver button, centre braid, and (unofficial) officers' edge-piping. The M1943 ROA field-grey pointed shoulder straps are piped red, with silver-braid rank bars. He displays a light grey German breast-eagle (permitted 15 Apr 1944); the ROA arm shield (still on the left sleeve for non-KONR troops); and the buttonhole-ribbon of the Eastern Decoration 2nd Class in Silver. His light field equipment and weapons are standard German issue.

D: KONR ARMED FORCES, 1945

D1: *Ober-yefreytor*, 1601st Grenadier Regiment; Erlenhof, April 1945

This deputy section commander attacking the Soviet bridgehead wears an M1943 peaked field cap with a ROA enlisted ranks' red-and-blue badge. His M1942 wide-collared greatcoat has M1943 ROA dark bluish-green shoulder straps piped red, with a silver star on the rank bar. The M1943 ROA arm shield was worn on the right sleeve by the KONR divisions. He carries a Kar 98k rifle and a Panzerfaust 60 anti-tank weapon.

D2: *Podporuchik*, 8th Night Intruder Squadron; Eger, Bohemia-Moravia, March 1945

This commissioned flight wireless operator of the operational Junkers Ju 88 unit wears the M1935 Luftwaffe officers' grey-blue service cap with the swastika cut off the silver-wire eagle badge (as ordered 2 March 1945), and an M1943 ROA officers' cockade. His flight blouse has German shoulder and collar rank insignia (ordered 18 March 1944) with golden-yellow flying-branch colour; an M1935 officers' breast-eagle also without the swastika; an M1943 ROA arm shield, worn on the right sleeve by the VVS-KONR like other KONR personnel; a ribbon bar of the Iron Cross 2nd Class and Eastern Decoration 2nd Class in Bronze; the M1936 Wireless Operator/Air Gunner's qualification badge, and a silver M1939 Wound Badge. His M1940 'Channel' flight trousers are tucked into M1937 flying boots, and he carries an LKP S100 brown-linen summer flying helmet with intercom connection.

D3: *Mayor*, 1603rd Grenadier Regiment; Prague, May 1945

This battalion commander wears a German service cap with white infantry piping, silver cords, and the ROA officers' badge. The M1935 tunic has a dark bluish-green collar and collar patches, with silver button, piping and braid; German shoulder straps with white underlay; a German M1935 officers' breast-eagle; and the M1943 ROA arm shield on the right sleeve. On his right breast pocket is the Officers' Academy graduation badge, on the left the star of the Eastern Decoration 1st Class in Silver, above that pocket the 2nd Class ribbon, and in his buttonhole the German ribbon for the Eastern Winter 1941/42 Medal. Note around his left sleeve a narrow ribbon in white-blue-red Russian national colours, indicating the 1st KONR Div's attempted last-minute switch of allegiance to the Allies.

E: COSSACKS IN THE CAUCASUS CAMPAIGN, 1942–43

E1: *Pod'esaul*, Cossack cavalry squadron, German 4th Mountain Division; Donetsk, March 1942

This Kuban Cossack squadron commander wears traditional Caucasian uniform for a ceremonial occasion. The *kubanka* cap has a red crown with elaborate silver braiding, and a German Army white-metal eagle-and-swastika badge. The brown *cherkeska* coat has sets of nine cartridge-holders, appropriate to his rank; Tsarist *pogoni* shoulder straps in silver braid with red piping and four gold rank stars; a German silver-wire breast-eagle; and an M1939 Mountain Troops right-arm badge from his parent division. The coat is worn over a white *beshmet* shirt with tiny ball-buttons, royal-blue *sharovary* breeches and soft leather riding boots. The *pojas* belt, with decorated hanging straps, supports a Caucasian M1904 *kindzhal* dagger, a *shashqa* sword and an M1895 revolver, and a *naigaka* whip is tucked under it.

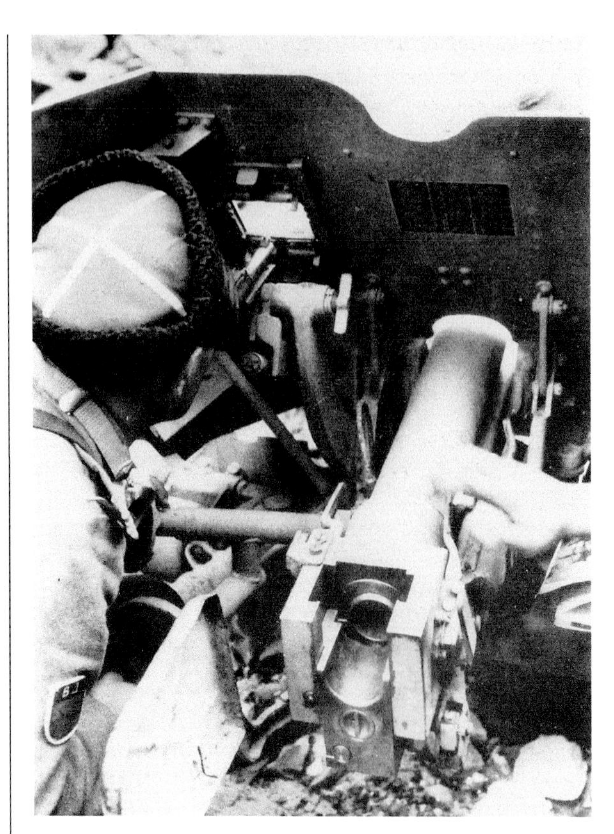

A junior officer of 1st Don Cossack Regt peers through the gunshield vision slit of a 7.5cm *leichtes Infanteriegeschütz 18*, usually issued two per battalion. The red cloth crown of his black lambswool *papacha* cap is decorated with a silver- or gold-braid cross, and his M1943 Don Cossack service-quality silver-braid shoulder straps have red edge-piping and a blue centre-stripe. His 5th-pattern Don Cossack arm shield is worn on the right upper sleeve for the 1st Regiment. (Tchakov Collection)

E2: *Zugführer*, Platov Cossack Regiment, German 17th Army; Maikop, July 1942

This platoon commander wears German uniform, with an M1938 officers' field cap piped silver at the crown and red in the front 'scoop' of the flap, and a German red (inner)-white-black cockade. The M1940 enlisted ranks' field-grey tunic has M1942 Cossack officers' white shoulder straps, a German M1935 officers' breast-eagle, and Security units' silver-braided red collar patches. He has reinforced breeches and riding boots, a German officers' field belt with a holstered Luger P08 pistol, and a Red Army M1926 Cossack *shashqa* sword hanging from the usual narrow cross-strap.

E3: *Stellvertretender Gruppenführer*, 7th Cossack Police Squadron; February 1943

This junior NCO serves in a German Police (Schutzpolizei) squadron attached to the Von Jungschultz Cavalry Regiment. His *kubanka* cap has an Imperial German cavalry 'Brunswick skull' badge. He wears a new M1943 Police 'field-grey' tunic (of a greyer shade than Army field-grey), with M1942 green-piped shoulder straps with a rank bar, and 'Ls' of rank braid on M1942 Police collar patches. The regimental skull-and-crossbones badge is worn on a yellow-edged black patch below the M1943 Police-green arm badge; the 'Prussian skull' on a black shield or diamond were alternatives. He has an M1936 Police enlisted men's belt with pouches for the Kar 98k rifle.

F: COSSACK UNITS, 1943–44

F1: *Khorunzhiy* Isayev, 360th Fortress Grenadier Regiment; Royan, France, April 1944

This Don Cossack second-lieutenant wears a German M1942 enlisted ranks' field cap with an M1942 Cossack badge of crossed lances on a red bar on a bluish-green oval patch; note his hair styled in a *chub* quiff at the temple. He has added a dark bluish-green collar to his M1943 tunic, and wears M1942 officers' silver-edged crossed-lances collar patches, M1943 Don Cossack service-dress shoulder straps, and the German officers' breast-eagle. The left-sleeve badges are regimental: the large tin 'tank and F', above a red 'Old French' shield with an inset silver edge. Depicted on some formal occasion, he wears three Eastern Decorations 2nd Class: for Bravery in Gold with Swords, for Merit in Silver, and for Merit in Bronze. Below these are a bronze M1939 Tank Battle Badge for AFV service, and a silver Wound Badge (for 3–4 wounds).

Medals After initial reluctance, Hitler permitted the award of the War Merit Cross and Iron Cross in both classes to Eastern Troops and Cossacks. They were also eligible for the Eastern Winter Campaign 1941/42 Medal *('Ost-Medaille')*; and for war badges such as the M1939 Wound Badge, M1939 Infantry Assault Badge, M1940 General Assault Badge, M1942 Anti-Partisan War Badge, and the M1942 Tank Destruction Badge worn on the right sleeve. On 14 July 1942 the Bravery & Merit Decoration (usually called the 'Eastern People's Decoration') was introduced specifically for such troops, though it was also made available from Nov 1942 to German cadre personnel. It comprised a rosette within an eight-point star for good conduct, and with added crossed swords for bravery. The 1st Class award was a pin-back star on the left breast pocket, and the 2nd Class a medal worn on a ribbon above that pocket, or a ribbon fixed diagonally through the second front buttonhole of the field uniform. There were five levels: 1st Class in Gold – gold star; 1st Class in Silver – silver star; 2nd Class in Gold – gold star, green ribbon with narrow red inner edge-stripes; 2nd Class in Silver – silver star, green ribbon with narrow white inner edge-stripes; 3rd Class in Bronze – bronze star, plain green ribbon. The 2nd Class medals could be awarded to an individual up to three times. When worn on a breast bar, the green ribbon for bravery awards bore small crossed swords.

F2: *Generalmajor* Helmuth von Pannwitz, GOC 1st Cossack Division; Hrvatska Mitrovica, Croatia, September 1943

Pannwitz wears his Bodyguard Mounted Squadron's parade uniform with a badgeless white Don *papacha* cap, braided in gold on its red crown. His red *beshmet* shirt has general officers' wide silver edging-braid. The black *cherkeska* has silver cuff braiding, and the German general officers' plaited gold-wire shoulder straps and gold-wire breast-eagle. He wears a red *bashlyk* hood behind the shoulders, and carries a holstered Luger P08 pistol, a private-purchase *kindzhal* dagger with a horn hilt, and an M1926 *shashqa* sword; note too the gold-cord lanyards. Around his neck hangs his Knight's Cross with Oak Leaves, awarded 23 Dec 1942.

F3: *Hauptwachtmeister*, 11th Kuban Cossack Regiment; Belarus, September 1943

This squadron sergeant-major wears an M1941 tunic with M1942 Cossack enlisted ranks' crossed-lances collar patches and (unofficial) German NCO collar braid; Kuban Cossack red shoulder straps with silver-braid rank bars; an M1942 'winged swastika' breast badge; and an M1942 Kuban arm shield quartered diagonally in yellow and green (normally seen on the left sleeve, but here on the right). The two NCO-braid cuff rings and the report book tucked into his tunic indicate his status as squadron sergeant-major, and he displays two ribbons of the Eastern People's Decoration 2nd Class in Silver. His outfit is completed by a plain helmet, belt and woollen gloves, Kuban Cossack breeches with 2.5cm red stripes, and riding boots.

G: 1st COSSACK DIVISION; CROATIA, 1943–44

G1: *Unteroffizier*, Bodyguard Mounted Squadron; Fruška Gora, October 1943

This guardsman wears a black *kubanka* cap with a red cloth crown and gold-braid cross. His M1935 tunic has a dark bluish-green collar with NCO-braid edging and M1942 enlisted ranks' crossed-lances patches. The M1943 red-piped dark bluish-green shoulder straps have gold-braid rank bars; other distinctions of this squadron are gold cuff chevrons, and on the right sleeve an oval blue cloth badge depicting a gold Ataman's mace between two *shashqa* swords. An early recruit to the Germans, he sports the buttonhole-ribbon of the Eastern Winter 1941/42 Medal.

G2: *Oberleutnant*, 6th Terek Cossack Mounted Regiment; Doboj, November 1943

This German cadre squadron commander wears a black *kubanka* cap with a Terek cornflower-blue crown braided with a silver cross, and German service-cap insignia. His officers' tunic has conventional cavalry collar patches and shoulder straps of rank, and on his left sleeve a 4th-pattern Terek arm shield. His ribbon bar shows the Iron Cross 2nd Class, Eastern Decoration 2nd Class in Silver with Swords, and the Winter 1941/42 Medal. Below are three pin-back awards: the Iron Cross 1st Class, General Assault Badge, and a silver Wound Badge.

G3: *Sotnik*, II/55 Cossack Artillery Battalion; Prnjavor, January 1944

This battery commander wears a red-crowned *kubanka* cap with a silver-braid cross, and a German Army eagle above the M1943 officers' red-black-silver cockade. Again, note the *cholka* hairstyle. The M1943 dark bluish-green shoulder straps were prescribed for the M1942 wide-collar greatcoat, on which officers commonly wore the M1942 enlisted ranks' crossed-lances patches, but the greatcoat displays no arm shield. He wears a German officers' belt, and carries binoculars and case and a P08 pistol. He also carries by choice the sturdy Soviet PPSh41 sub-machine gun.

H: COSSACK CAVALRY CORPS; CROATIA, 1944–45

H1: *Starshiy Prikasni*, 4th Kuban Cossack Mounted Regiment; Valpovo, March 1945

This section machine-gunner wears German uniform and insignia, except for the M1943 Kuban cockade on his field cap, and the 5th-pattern Kuban arm shield on his right sleeve. His M1940 tunic has shoulder straps with cavalry-yellow piping, an M1940 breast-eagle and collar patches, and M1940 left-sleeve rank chevrons. Although they are obscured here, his M1940 trousers have 2.5cm red stripes. He also wears the standard belt kit for an MG42 gunner.

H2: *Polkovnik* Ivan N. Kononov, 5th Don Cossack Mounted Regiment; Virovitica, January 1945

Kononov wears a Don Cossack red-crowned *papacha* cap with a German M1935 metal eagle and M1943 Don officers' cockade. His German M1935 officers' tunic has the regulation collar patches and plaited shoulder straps of his branch and rank, and a silver-wire breast-eagle. On his left sleeve is a 5th-pattern Don Cossack arm shield, below an improvised Cossack proficiency badge – here a strip of silver German NCO *Tresse*, instead of the regulation gold braid. At his throat he wears the Croatian Order of King Zvonimir's Crown 1st Class with Oak Wreath, and on his left breast pocket the Iron Cross 1st Class. His field-grey breeches have Don Cossack 5cm red stripes, and his sword knot is red, gold and silver.

H3: *Kazak*, 2nd Siberian Cossack Mounted Regiment; Nova Gradiška, September 1944

This trooper's shaggy white Siberian *kubanka* cap with a yellow crown was often worn without a badge. He wears a Panzer troops' grey collared shirt; the M1943 khaki tropical tunic has integral collar patches, but an added breast-eagle, and M1943 ROA dark bluish-green shoulder straps piped red. On the left sleeve is an M1943 Siberian host arm shield, and his royal-blue breeches have 5cm yellow stripes. He wears a Russian belt with German pouches, and carries an M1926 *shashqa* sword and a slung Kar 98k rifle.

INDEX

References to illustration captions are shown in **bold**. Plates are shown with page and caption locators in brackets.

Abwehr (Army Intelligence) 15, 16, 19
ammunition 5, **7**, 44
armbands 5, **6**, 12, 14, 15, 18, 44
Ataman 22, 34, 35, 36, 37
Ataman's mace 38, 43, 47; Field Ataman 39, 40
Austria 20, 37, 39, 40

Baltic States, the 3, 6, 15
bashlyk hood **20**, 21, **23**, **38**, 47
Belarus 3, 5, **6**, **8**, 9, 10, 11, 13, 14, 16, 17, 19, 21, 23, **C27**, **F30**, 34, 35, 36, 39, **44**, 45, 47
breeches **23**, 39, 46, 47
royal blue 17, 21, 23, 39, 44, 45, 47; *sharovary* **4**, **6**, 17, 45
Britain 14, **34**, 40
British Army, the 41, 42
8th Army 4, 37, 40

Caucasus, the 20, 21, 22, **E29**, 35, 45
cherkeska coat **20**, 21, **38**, 45, 47
chevrons 7, **21**, 22, 23, 38, 40, 41, 42, 47
civilians 3, **4**, 5, 18, 19, 21, 34, 36, 40
cockades **8**, 14, 15, **16**, **17**, **21**, **22**, **24**, **33**, 38, 40, **44**, 45, 46, 47
collars **7**, 12, 15, **17**, **21**, 22, 23, **24**, **33**, 38, 40, **44**, 45, 46, 47
braid **6**, 23, 47; patches **4**, 5, **6**, **7**, **8**, 10, 12, 14, **15**, **16**, **17**, **18**, 20, **21**, **22**, **23**, **24**, **33**, **39**, 40, 41, 42, **44**, 45, 46, 47
Cossack Settlement (*Kazachi Stan*) 34, 36, **39**
Cossacks 4, 6, 10, 11, 13, 15, **18**, **20**, **21**, 22, **23**, **24**, **E29**, **F30**, **G31**, **H32**, **33**, **34**, 35, 36, 37, 38, **39**, 40, 42, 45, 46, 47
regiments: Don 3, 7, 20, **21**, **22**, **23**, **24**, **H32**, **33**, 34, 35, 36, 37, 38, 39, 40, 43, **46**, 47; Kuban **20**, 21, 22, **23**, 24, **F30**, **H32**, 33, 34, 35, 36, 37, 38, 39, 40, 43, 45, 47; Platov 22, 23, **E29**, 35, 46; Siberian 20, 23, **H32**, 35, 37, 38, 39, 43, 47; Terek 20, 21, 22, 23, **24**, **G31**, 33, 34, 35, 36, 38, 39, 40, 43, 47; Volga 22, 34, 35; Von Jungschultz 22, **23**, 35, 43, 46; Pannwitz Mtd Unit 22, 34, 35; 1st Cossack Division *(1.Kozaken-Division)* 21, **G31**, 34, 47; Cossack Cavalry Corps **H32**, 34, 35, 37, **39**, 47; Independent Cossack Corps (*Otdel'niy Kazachiy Korpus*) 36, 40
Croatia 3, **F30**, **G31**, **H32**, **33**, 34, 35, 36, 37, **38**, **39**, 47

Denmark 9, 10, 11, 12, 13
deserters 5, 16, 19, 34

eagles **21**, 22, **23**, **33**, 45, 47
breast-eagle 5, **6**, **7**, **8**, 15, **18**, 20, 22, **24**, **33**, 45, 46, 47; eagle-and-swastika **8**, 12, 13, 15, 22, **24**, 38, 40, 45
Eastern Front, the 11, 15, 34, 36
Erlenhof 14, 15, **D28**, 45

field caps **4**, 24, 44, 47
kubanka **18**, **20**, **21**, 22, **23**, **24**, **38**, 40, 45, 46, 47; M1934 **8**, 22, **33**, 44; M1938 7, 46; M1942 **6**, **8**, **11**, 46; M1943 **6**, 15, **18**, 40, 45; *papacha* **21**, **22**, **23**, **24**, **33**, 38, 40, **46**, 47; *pilotka* **16**, **17**, 44
field shirts 11, **17**
beshmet **20**; khaki **4**, **6**, **24**; M1929 44; M1935 **4**, **6**, **16**, 17, **33**

France 7, **8**, 9, 10, 11, 12, 13, 14, 22, **F30**, **34**, 35, 36, 37, 46

German Army 5, **8**, 19, 20, 36, 37, 40, 41, 42, 45, 47
Army Group 4, 5, 8; 'A' 21; 'B' 21; Centre 6, 13, 21, 35; North 3, 21, 23; Rear Area 3, 4, 5, 13, 16, 19, 21, 22, 35; South 3, 6, 23
Germany 9, 10, 11, 12, 13, 34, 35, 36, 39
greatcoats 23, **33**, 38, 44, 45, 47

headgear 12, 17, 22, 40
helmets **6**, 7, 17, 22, 45, 47
Hilfswillige/Hiwi (army auxiliaries) **4**, 5, 7, 8, 12, 13, 14, 21, **A25**, 44
Hitler, Adolf 3, 4, 5, 8, 11, 21, 36, 46

insignia **4**, 5, **7**, 8, 10, **11**, 12, 15, **17**, 19, 20, **21**, 22, 23, **24**, 33, 37, **38**, **39**, 41, 42, **44**, 45, 47
Italy 9, 10, 11, 12, 22, 34, 35, 36, **39**, 40

Kaminski, Bronisław V. 6, 18, 19, **44**
Kaminski Brigade **18**, 44
kindzhal dagger **20**, **38**, 45, 47
Kononov, *Podpolkovnik* Ivan N. 21, 24, **H32**, **33**, 35, 37, 47

Luftwaffe, the 4, 14, **15**, 16, 45

machine guns:
7.62mm M1928 Degtyaryov **3**; MP40 sub-machine gun **6**, 44; Soviet PPSh-41 sub-machine gun **6**, **39**, 47
Moscow 3, **6**, **11**, 14, 15, **34**, 38, 40

non-commissioned officers (NCOs) **6**, **7**, **21**, **22**, 23, 24, 33, **38**, 41, 42, 44, 46, 47
Normandy 3, 5, 10, 11, 12, **C27**, 34, 45

Oder Front, the 13, 14, 19
Osintorf 16, **A25**, 44

Pannwitz, *General-mayor* Helmuth von 22, **F30**, 34, 35, 36, 37, 38, 40, 47
partisans 5, 6, 16, 17, 18, 19, 23, 36, 37, 39, 40
anti-partisan 6, 13, 14, 16, 17, 18, 19
Plastun (Cossack infantry) 21, 23, 24, **34**, 35, 36, 37, 39, 40
pojas belt **20**, 21, 45
Poland 9, 10, 11, 18, 19, 20, 24, 34, 39, 43
pouches **7**, **39**, 44, 45, 46, 47
Prague **12**, 13, 14, **D28**, 45
prisoners of war (POWs) 4, 5, 7, 13, 14, 16, 17, 19, 22, 34
Pskov **17**, 18, 19, **B26**, **C27**, 44, 45

rank bars 7, **8**, 17, **21**, 23, **24**, 38, 44, 45, 46, 47
ranks: *Feldwebel* **B26**, **33**, 41, 44; *General-mayor* **12**, 20, **F30**, 35, 37, 39, 41, 42; *General der Osttruppen im OKH* (General Officer Commanding - GOC) 3, 4, 10, 21, 35, 47; *Hauptfeldwebel* **6**, 7, 41; *Hauptwachtmeister* **F30**, 42, 47; *Kapitan* **A25**, 41, 44; *Kazak* **H32**, 42, 47; *Khorunzhiy* **F30**, **38**, 42, 46; *Kompanieführer* **A25**, 41, 44; *Mayor* 16, 17, **D28**, **33**, 41, 42, 45; *Oberleutnant* **G31**, 47; *Ober-yefreytor* **D28**, 41, 45; *Podpolkovnik* **17**, 19, 21, 35, 41; *Podporuchik* **15**, **18**, **B26**, **D28**, 41, 44, 45; *Polkovnik* **12**, 14, 16, 18, **H32**, 37, 39, 41, 42, 47; *Sonderführer* (Specialist Officer) 7, 16, 23, 24; *Sotnik* **G31**, 42, 47; *Starshiy Prikasni* **H32**, 42, 47; *Stellvertretender Gruppenführer* 24, **E29**, 41, 42, 46; *Unteroffizier* 5, **24**, **B26**, **G31**, 41, 42, 44, 47; *Zugführer* 7, **21**, 23, 24, **E29**, 41, 42, 46
Red Army, the 3, **4**, 5, **6**, 7, 14, **16**, 17, 18, 19, 20, 21, 23, **24**, **33**, 34, 37, 39, **44**, 46
Regulation: 1200/43 11; 8000/42 7, 23; 10650/42 24; 141242/43 10, 24; 32003/44 12, 15, 33
riding boots 17, **18**, **23**, **39**, 45, 46, 47
Russia/Soviet Union/USSR, the 3, 4, 5, **6**, 7, **8**, 9, 10, 11, 12, 13, 14, 15, 16, **17**, 18, 19, 20, 21, 22, 23, 33, 35, 36, 38, 40, 41, 42, 44, 45, 47
Russian Liberation Army (*ROA*) **3**, 4, **8**, 9, 10, **11**, **12**, 13, 14, **15**, **16**, **17**, **18**, 19, 20, 24, **B26**, **34**, **39**, 41, **44**, 45, 47
Eastern Battalions (Bns), the **3**, 7, **8**, 9, 12, 13, 15, 23, 24, 44, 45
Russian Liberation People's Army (*RONA*) **18**, 19, **B26**, **44**
Russian Nationalist People's Army (*RNNA*) 6, 10, **16**, **17**, 18, **A25**, 41, 44
Russian People's Liberation Committee (*KONR*) **3**, 4, **12**, 13, 14, 15, 19, 20, **D28**, **34**, 45
Russian People's Liberation Committee Air Force (*VVS-KONR*) 14, 15, 45
Russian People's Liberation Committee Armed Forces (*VS-KONR*) 12, 13, 37
Russian volunteer units 4, 15, **A25**, **B26**, 44

shashqa sword **20**, **23**, 38, 45, 46, 47
shields 8, 15, 19, 24, **33**, **34**, 38, **39**, 40, 46
arm **8**, 11, **12**, **15**, **18**, 19, 20, **24**, 34, 38, 39, 43, **44**, 45, **46**, 47; M1943 *ROA* **8**, 11, **12**, 13, 14, **15**, **17**, **18**, 34, 44, 45
shoulder straps **4**, 5, **6**, **7**, 10, 11, 14, **15**, **16**, 17, **18**, **22**, 23, **24**, **33**, **38**, **39**, 40, 41, 42, **44**, 45, 47
M1940 **8**, 23, **24**; M1942 **7**, **17**, 44, 46; M1943 **8**, **17**, **18**, 24, 38, 45, **46**, 47; *pogoni* 10, 21, 45; *RNNA* **17**, 44; *ROA* **16**, **17**, 45
Special Div–Russia *(Sonderdivision R)* 19, 20, **B26**
SS Intelligence (Sicherheitsdienst - SD) 15, 17, 19, 44, 45
St Andrew's Cross 5, 8, 15
Stalin, Joseph 3, 4, 7, 8, 21
Stalingrad 3, 5, 7, 11, 34
swastikas 7, 15, 45
winged 11, 22, 24, **33**, 44, 47

tanks 13, 19, 34, 45
T-34 13, 14, 19
Trukhin, *General-mayor* Fedor I. **12**, 13, 14
tunics 12, 15, 21, 22, **24**, 33, 45, 47
field **4**, **21**, 22, **23**, 38, **44**; M1932 **4**; M1934 23; M1935 **6**, **7**, **18**, **21**, **22**, **23**, **33**, 45, 47; M1937 44; M1940 **6**, **7**, **18**, 22, **23**, 40, 46, 47; M1941 22, **39**, 40, 44, 47; M1943 **8**, 22, 40, 44, 45, 46, 47

Ukraine 3, 4, 5, 6, **8**, 9, 10, 11, 12, 19, 20, 21, 22, 23, 34, 35, 36
uniforms **3**, 5, 7, **8**, 10, **11**, **12**, 14, **15**, **16**, 17, **18**, 19, 20, 21, 22, 23, 24, **33**, **34**, 37, **38**, 40, 44, 45, 46, 47

Vlasov, *GenLt* Andrey A. **3**, 5, **7**, 8, **12**, 14, **C27**, 37, 45

war badges **15**, 44, 46
Warsaw **18**, 19
Uprising 19, 34, 35, 36
Wehrmacht, the 3, 4, 5, 11, 12, 44

Zhilenkov, *General-leytenant* Georgiy N. **12**, 14, 16, 18, **C27**, 45